THE COMMERCIAL LEASE GUIDEBOOK

Learn How To Win The Leasing Game!

Thomas G. Mitchell

The Commercial Lease Guidebook

Learn how to win the leasing game!

© 1992 by THOMAS G. MITCHELL

Illustrations by John Heacock
Book design and typesetting by Warren Jessop

Published by
MACORE International
P.O. BOX 10811
LAHAINA, MAUI, HAWAII 96761
First edition 1992
Second printing 1999
Third printing 2001
Library of Congress Cataloging in Publication Number: 92-80954

ISBN 0-9632982-0-8

SAN 297-6609

ACKNOWLEDGMENTS

TO MY DAD
who convinced me I could do
whatever I really wanted to do. . .

TO MY DEAR FRIEND JK
who simply has long been my dear friend. . .

TO CECIL COMPTON
who had enough courage to hire me
into commercial real estate. . .

TO TOM TOWE
who helped me a lot when
I first got started. . .

TO BILL CURTIS
who was my first partner. . .

TO MY TENANTS AND CLIENTS
without whom I wouldn't have been
able to write this book. . .

TO MY SON ERIK
who is just starting his real estate career. . .

TO WARREN JESSOP
whose dedication and patience have made
this an eminently more readable book. . .

AND TO LYNDA DONATO
who encouraged me to do what I really
wanted to. . . she's so special!!!

*MAHALO AND ALOHA
TO ALL OF YOU!!!*

ABOUT THE AUTHOR

 Thomas G. Mitchell is a 1967 graduate of the University of Cincinnati's College of Business Administration, and has done graduate work at the University of Cincinnati, Ohio, and at Santa Clara University in California. He has been active in all phases of brokerage, development, and property management since 1975.

As a real estate practitioner in California and Hawaii, he has negotiated literally hundreds of commercial and industrial leases on well over a million square feet of space. He has also negotiated dozens of sales transactions on land, office, retail and industrial buildings, as well as on numerous residential properties.

Mr. Mitchell has served as a managing general partner for over a dozen development projects in several states in which he was responsible for marketing and leasing. He was also active in financing and construction negotiations, and in partnership administration.

In 1979, he founded his investment firm, Mitchell and Company Real Estate, Inc. (MACORE) . In the early 1980s he developed a computer software package called the "Real Estate Development System" (REDS). He is currently president of Elite Properties, Inc., a diversified residential and commercial real estate firm in Lahaina, Maui, Hawaii.

TABLE OF CONTENTS

AN ANECDOTE

PRIDE AND PRINCIPLE

ONCE UPON A TIME, IN THE LUCRATIVE LAND OF BUSINESS, A CRAFTSMAN WAS BORN. THIS CRAFTSMAN WAS NAMED "PRIDE." AS HIS SKILL DEVELOPED, AND HIS TECHNIQUES WERE PERFECTED, PRIDE'S REPUTATION IMPROVED QUICKLY. PEOPLE BEGAN TO NOTICE HIS WORK, AND OFTEN PRAISED HIM ON ITS QUALITY.

THIS MOTIVATED PRIDE TO WORK EVEN HARDER. HE CONCENTRATED ON PERFECTING THE TECHNIQUES THAT PEOPLE PRAISED THE MOST. ONE DAY, SOMEONE CAME ALONG AND OFFERED TO BUY SOMETHING PRIDE MADE. HE WAS ELATED BY HIS SUCCESS, AND PRIDE GREW ENORMOUSLY.

HE DECIDED TO MAKE MORE ARTICLES FOR SALE. WHEN HE DISCOVERED THAT PEOPLE REALLY WANTED HIS STUFF FASTER THAN HE COULD CREATE IT, HE STARTED RAISING HIS PRICES. THEN HE MADE ANOTHER AMAZING DISCOVERY. PEOPLE DIDN'T SEEM TO MIND THE LOFTY PRICES AS LONG AS HIS WORK WAS GOOD. THIS MADE PRIDE FEEL VERY COMFORTABLE AND SECURE.

ONE DAY ANOTHER PERSON CAME ALONG AND WANTED PRIDE TO MAKE SOMETHING HE HAD ALREADY CREATED FOR SOMEONE ELSE. NOW PRIDE REALLY SWELLED. HE FELT KIND OF BAD ABOUT LOWERING THE VALUE OF THE PIECE HE HAD SOLD TO THE FIRST PERSON, BUT HE FIGURED HE DESERVED THE MONEY SO HE DID IT ANYWAY. THIS

INSPIRED YET ANOTHER DISCOVERY. PRIDE DECIDED TO START MAKING THINGS THAT HE COULD DUPLICATE AND THEN SELL TO A WHOLE BUNCH OF PEOPLE. "THINK OF THE PROFITS!" PRIDE SAID TO HIMSELF.

PRIDE QUICKLY PILED UP A BUNCH OF STUFF TO SELL, BUT NOT ENOUGH PEOPLE STROLLED BY HIS PLACE. WELL, PRIDE WAS A PRETTY SMART GUY. HE DECIDED TO GO OUT AND FIND A BETTER PLACE TO SELL HIS STUFF.

NOT WANTING TO TAKE TOO MUCH TIME AWAY FROM HIS CRAFT, PRIDE DECIDED TO USE GOBETWEEN TO FIND HIM A NEW PLACE. GOBETWEEN KNEW EXACTLY THE PLACE FOR PRIDE. IT WAS A PLACE ON THE MAIN ROAD IN TOWN THAT PRACTICALLY EVERYBODY WENT BY, AND IT WAS OWNED BY "PRINCIPLE," A PRETTY STERN BUT FAIR-MINDED INDIVIDUAL.

PRINCIPLE HAD HEARD OF PRIDE'S WORK AND WAS ANXIOUS TO RENT SOME SPACE TO PRIDE SO THEY COULD BOTH PROSPER. GOBETWEEN QUICKLY ARRANGED A MEETING, AND THEY ALL AGREED ON A DEAL. WHILE GOBETWEEN WAS BUSY WRITING DOWN THE TERMS OF THE DEAL, PRIDE STARTED WONDERING IF HE HAD BEEN A BIT HASTY. HE STARTED THINKING OF LITTLE WAYS TO MAKE THE DEAL MORE PROFITABLE FOR HIMSELF. HE TOLD GOBETWEEN TO WRITE IN THE CHANGES HE THOUGHT OF.

GOBETWEEN WASN'T CRAZY ABOUT DOING THIS BECAUSE HE KNEW OF PRINCIPLE'S FAIR-MINDED REPUTATION, AND WORRIED THAT THIS MIGHT SEEM A BIT UNSCRUPULOUS ESPECIALLY SINCE HE HADN'T MENTIONED THE CHANGES TO PRINCIPLE. BUT GOBETWEEN FIGURED HE WAS NOTHING BUT A MIDDLE MAN, SO HE PUT THEM IN ANYWAY.

PRINCIPLE ANXIOUSLY READ THE CONTRACT, BUT WAS PUZZLED. HE COMPARED THE CONTRACT TO HIS MEETING NOTES, AND WHEN HE UNCOVERED THE DISCREPANCIES, PRINCIPLE WAS DOWNRIGHT OFFENDED!

FORTUNATELY, GOBETWEEN HAD BEEN THROUGH THINGS LIKE THIS BEFORE, AND MANAGED TO SETTLE PRINCIPLE DOWN, AND EVEN TO GO ALONG WITH SOME OF THE CHANGES, PLEADING THAT THERE SIMPLY MUST HAVE BEEN A MISUNDERSTANDING, NOT MALICE ON PRIDE'S PART. HE LEFT FEELING SMUG THAT HE HAD SMOOTHED THINGS OUT.

BUT WHEN PRIDE SAW THE CONCESSIONS PRINCIPLE HAD MADE, HE GOT EVEN MORE GREEDY AND SENT GOBETWEEN BACK WITH STILL MORE CHANGES.

WELL, THAT WAS IT. PRINCIPLE WAS OUTRAGED! CONVINCED THAT HE WAS DEALING WITH AN UNSCRUPULOUS SCOUNDREL, HE REFUSED TO REPLY TO PRIDE'S OFFER, AND SENT GOBETWEEN AWAY WITH A GOOD CHASTISING.

PRIDE WOUND UP BACK AT HIS ORIGINAL PLACE, AND PRINCIPLE RENTED THE SPACE TO ANOTHER CRAFTSMAN. GOBETWEEN WENT AWAY EMPTY-HANDED OF COURSE, AND RELUCTANTLY LOOKED FOR ANOTHER PLACE FOR PRIDE.

BUT IT WAS HARD TO FIND A PLACE FOR PRIDE IN THE LAND OF BUSINESS; AND PRINCIPLE NEVER DID NEARLY AS WELL AS HE MIGHT HAVE.

AND THE MORAL OF THE STORY IS. . .

WELL, I THINK YOU GET THE PICTURE. . .

PREFACE

As I was growing up, I used to walk around downtown
Cincinnati staring up at the 52-story Carew Tower, wondering
how anyone could ever manage to own a building like that. I
became obsessed with the idea of learning how those buildings
came to be, and how commercial real estate was actually trans-
acted.

In July 1976, I became a commercial real estate salesman in
California, and a broker in 1978. I was fortunate to have been
involved at the inception (and the subsequent explosion) of the
now-famous "Silicon Valley," in the South Bay Area of San
Francisco. Silicon Valley has now become to the electronics
industry what Detroit is to the auto industry.

I kept a log of every deal I made, and by September 1981, my
log contained 122 leases. The log stops there, but I remained
very active. I have negotiated several hundred office, industrial,
and retail leases, as both a broker and as a landlord (I became a
developer in 1979).

I learned early on that the lease is the backbone of commercial
real estate deals. It is an incredibly powerful document. It
creates a profound economic impact on the parties signing it. It
dictates the landlord's financing. It is a binding legal contract
that controls the tenant's physical conduct on the property. It
can apply to a few hundred square feet, or to acres of buildings
under roof, or to sections of land. Landlord's who fail to con-
summate timely lease deals can, and often do, lose their properties in foreclosure actions.

*Properly done, the commercial lease
becomes a passive and sleepy document.*

Yet properly done, the commercial lease becomes a passive and sleepy document. In my experience, the vast majority of leases were slipped into the file drawer upon execution, and removed upon expiration.

For most people, reading a commercial lease is comparable to watching paint dry. It's not very exciting to do unless you are studying for some sort of test, or are earning good money for doing it.

Throughout my career, I have noticed how uncomfortable many business people are with a commercial lease document. Even people *active* in commercial real estate! The problem is that *the language of leases is foreign to most people.* How exciting can it be to read something written in a language you don't understand?

Without an interpreter, and an organized approach, plowing through scores of pages replete with legal jargon can be agonizing! But not a great deal has been written about how to read or how to understand the commercial lease, which is the reason I decided to write this book.

The approach I use took me a decade-and-a-half to figure out! To save you some agony, I've tried to present my techniques in a way that the "lay person," as well as the real estate professional, can easily handle.

The unfortunate and confusing thing about the world of leases is that there is no standard for naming lease provisions, and no set order for placing them in the lease. The same provision can have any number of names in different leases, and can occur in any order from one lease to another. It just depends on who drafted it. Look now at "Exhibit A" and you'll see exactly what I mean.

Preface

I spent a lot of time studying the tables of contents and the clauses of dozens of commercial leases. I have summarized provisions common to most leases into "GROUPS," and reviewed them from both the landlord's and the tenant's point of view. The "legalese" has been stripped away and replaced with plain language anyone can understand.

The "GROUP" technique I developed is the backbone of this book. In whatever order clauses appear in the lease you are reviewing, or whatever they are named, locating and grouping them in the order *I* use greatly simplifies the review process. Equally important, I also tell you how to go about the challenging job of *reading* a lease (without nodding off!).

My discussion of the parties' "positions" helps you understand the background for each provision. The plain language explanations will tell you what the provisions say, and therefore equip you to be a better negotiator. This is the key! Once you know *why* the lease says what it says, you *automatically* become a better negotiator. "Knowledge is power!" Make sense?

Here's another suggestion. As you read the chapters, each time you encounter a new term, take the time to look it up in the glossary, and perhaps again in the table of contents or the index. It's a pain, but if you want to understand what you are reading, you have to build your "commercial lease vocabulary."

"The Guidebook" is *not* a legal dictionary. It does not contain answers to every conceivable question about the commercial lease. The book *does* contain a concise discussion, in easy-to-understand language, of "commonly included provisions" found in most commercial leases. The objective is to give the reader a solid foundation for undertaking lease negotiations, based on an understanding of what the provisions say.

Whether you are involved as a landlord, tenant, lender, real estate or insurance broker, business consultant, or an attorney new to real estate, this book is bound to increase your understanding of the commercial lease, and therefore, help you through the negotiating process. For many commercial real estate specialists, this book will help you improve your negotiating skills by helping you remember things you have forgotten.

In short, this book will help you "learn how to win the leasing game"! We have a lot of ground to cover, so let's get started.

He who has the gold makes the rule. . .

INTRODUCTION

BACKGROUND FOR NEGOTIATIONS

The commercial lease is a great example of "The Gold Rule"—
he who has the gold makes the rule! Since the landlord owns the
property, the lease is designed primarily to protect the
landlord's property and ownership rights, and to satisfy the
requirements of a lending institution. Secondarily, the lease
defines the rights of the tenant.

It is this situation that sets up the need for "negotiation." The
landlord tries to maintain his legal and economic advantages,
while the tenant attempts to wrestle away some breathing
room. Consequently, if you are on the tenant's side of the
table, expect a "landlord-oriented" lease as you start your
review, and you will find it to be a lot less frustrating.

Whole books have been devoted to the art of "negotiating." It is
not the purpose of this book to duplicate those efforts. But I
will point out a few things specific to *lease* negotiations which
should be helpful.

If you are a tenant using an "agent" to conduct your
negotiations — meaning you are not *personally* participating in
the negotiation meetings — do yourself and your agent a favor.
Give the agent the proper negotiating tools. The agent needs
more than your company name and the size of your space
requirement. Your negotiator should be equipped with a
detailed list of specifications, budget restraints, critical dates,
names and titles of the parties who will sign the lease, and some
understanding of your financial situation. Your agent can then
make a much better impression on prospective landlords.

Likewise, landlords need to equip their agents with similar information.

The first step in the negotiation process is **setting objectives.** Never enter into negotiations without them! If you don't know where you're going, you're not likely to get there. Take the time to list your "needs" in their order of importance, and start negotiating from the top of your list.

Negotiation is the art of compromise. To conduct effective negotiations, you must distinguish your "needs" from your "wants." "Needs" are the things you absolutely must have in order to function. "Wants" are those extras that make life more pleasant. "You can't have everything." But you can try.

Bargain hard for your "needs," and don't be afraid to establish a bottom line on each issue. Create an agenda, and during the negotiating process, explain the reasons for the positions you take so as not to seem arbitrary. This will add to the other party's understanding of your situation, and will help develop your own credibility.

I refer to "wants" as "give-ups." Before you even start negotiating, prioritize your "give-ups," and sacrifice them carefully in exchange for "needs."

Understand that both parties have a "hidden agenda." It contains their list of "needs"—the points that will make or break the deal. It is camouflaged with "wants." Uncovering the other party's hidden agenda is, therefore, the key to success.

Here's an example. If you are a tenant and you *need* extra parking spaces (above the landlord's standard "parking ratio"), but you *want* a designated parking area, you will likely give-up the designated area in order to get the extra spaces you need.

Uncovering the other party's hidden agenda is the key to success.

Here are some other examples of

HIDDEN AGENDAS:

RENT:

Landlord's position

Stated Agenda:	"Base Rent" must be a certain amount.
Hidden Agenda:	My existing loan requires this amount in order to cover operating expenses and debt service; otherwise, I will lose money every month. . .
Stated Agenda:	"Percentage Rent" must be a certain amount. . .
Hidden Agenda:	My "Permanent Loan Commitment" requires that I achieve these amounts; otherwise the amount of the loan will be reduced, I will have to find alternate financing for the lost loan proceeds, AND times are the pits, AND oh my gosh. . .!

Tenant's position

Stated Agenda:	"Base Rent" cannot exceed a certain amount.
Hidden Agenda:	The home office established the rent budget, and I said "No problem"!
Stated Agenda:	"Percentage Rent" cannot exceed a certain amount. . .
Hidden Agenda:	Industry standards and/or experience dictate(s) that paying a higher percentage rent will force me into an operating loss.

TERM:

Landlord's Position

Stated Agenda:	The term has to start on a given date.
Hidden Agenda:	If the lease doesn't start by a given date, I'll miss another mortgage payment and the lender will foreclose on my loan!!!
Stated Agenda:	The lease can only be for a short term. . .
Hidden Agenda:	If the lease is for a long term, I'll have to pay a whopping brokerage commission!
Stated Agenda:	The lease must be for a long term. . .
Hidden Agenda:	If the lease is not for a long term, I won't fulfill the obligations under my loan commitment; or
	If I don't get a long-term lease now, I might have a vacancy right in the middle of next year's recession. . .!

Tenant's Position

Stated Agenda:	The term has to start on a given date.
Hidden Agenda:	Our existing lease expires next month, and we won't have a space if we can't move in by a given date!
Stated Agenda:	The lease cannot start until a given date.
Hidden Agenda:	Our investor walked out on us yesterday, and we are scrambling to find a new one, so we don't want the lease to start until a given date. . .
Stated Agenda:	The lease can only be for a short term. . .
Hidden Agenda:	We are not at all certain that our plan will work, so we only want a short term lease.

CONDEMNATION:

Landlord's position

Stated Agenda:	The entire condemnation award should go to the landlord.
Hidden Agenda:	The "Condemnation Notice" arrived last week!!!

USE:

Tenant's position

Stated Agenda:	We want the use broadly defined in case corporate headquarters decides to change strategy.
Hidden Agenda:	We have a secret idea that will enable us to dominate the market. If the landlord finds out, he will surely want a whole lot more rent!

✓ Be sure to negotiate your needs in the proper order! Sounds simple, I know, but it's easy to get caught up on a minor point and lose sight of the big picture. For example, don't spend a lot of time negotiating the "use" clause just to discover the property's zoning prohibits the use! Similarly, it makes little sense to dwell on the "security deposit" clause, if you have not resolved the "rent" issue!

Let me leave you with this thought. In the art of negotiating for your "needs" and "wants," *you are limited only by your imagination.* (See Exhibit E, "Ten Ways to Collect $5,000 per month for 36 months")

INTERFERENCE

Developing an appreciation for the other party's "needs and wants" is perhaps the most important ingredient to successful negotiating. This will become easier as you finish reading the following pages, because *you will learn the real issue underlying each lease provision.*

There are two things you have to do in order to discover the other party's position:

1) You must *ask* probing questions.
2) You must *listen* to the answers!

Asking questions is easy. Listening is not. But it is only by *really listening* that you develop a feel for the other party's "hidden agenda." If you don't deal with the hidden agenda, you seldom make the deal!

The secret to effective listening is to eliminate "interference" with what is being said verbally and through body language. You have to learn to screen out everything except what the other party is telling you, so you are able to read between the lines. It takes concentration.

Here is a practice exercise that will demonstrate the importance of the power of concentration. Sometime when you're just sitting around watching TV, sit the same distance from the TV that you would normally sit from people during negotiations. Turn the volume down to the level where you can barely hear it. Then, relax and try to listen to it while someone talks to you, or while some other noise occurs. Though you can still *hear* the TV, you will probably not be able to *understand* what's being said.

Now, without touching the TV, and with the same "interference" noise level, sit up, lean forward, and cup your hands behind your ears. Concentrate on the TV, not the noise. You will discover how much better you can hear the message. The only difference is your concentration level!

Similarly, when you lose your concentration during negotiations, you may hear a statement, yet completely miss its subtle meaning. This is the difference between uncovering someone's "hidden agenda" and totally missing the point! You must eliminate the interference when you're at the bargaining table. There is simply too much to lose if you don't!

As you listen to the other party's problems and begin to formulate solutions, you create an affirmative negotiating environment. You will wear away the adversarial relationship inherent in lease negotiations, and move closer to compromise. Believe me, eliminating interference—*really listening*— works!

POSTURING

Posturing is establishing the order of importance for your negotiating points based on your perception of the other party's priorities — the "hidden agenda." Posturing is one of the most interesting and challenging aspects of the negotiating process; in fact, it is the very essence of negotiation.

Figuring out what *you* really need or want is relatively easy, but it's another matter trying to out-guess the other party! Posturing involves creating a strategy to determine how to trade off your wants for your needs; how to sacrifice your less important needs or wants in exchange for your more important ones; or, how to accept one of the other party's points in exchange for gaining his acceptance of one of yours, and still wind up with the deal you wanted initially.

Your "negotiating posture" is created by your "stated motivation" for making the deal. Be sure to leave yourself some room to make concessions in the spirit of compromise. If you try to leave too much room, you may discourage or even offend the other party. If you don't allow enough room, you could leave money on the table. Your success at "posturing" will dictate your success in making the deal.

One of the most common questions asked about posturing is "what's normal?" The answer is "Nothing." Something reasonable for one landlord or tenant may be outrageous for another. Since you can't read a person's mind, you shouldn't be bashful about asking for utopia. The best negotiators are usually not afraid to be a bit "bodacious."

Nevertheless, you must remember that you are always dealing with *people* — human beings with feelings, wants, and needs. The best negotiators are also able to *develop a sensitivity to the other party's situation*. Deals occur only when both sides are satisfied that their needs have been met. "Normal," therefore, might be defined as the situation where both parties get enough of what they need to make the deal.

Here are a few "posturing" rules I try to follow:

- Don't violate the rules of common courtesy. Be pleasant but firm, and approach the negotiation with "positive expectancy." Your physical appearance and demeanor will not go unnoticed.

- Don't be afraid to establish your credentials, or to determine the other party's. Always try to negotiate with the ultimate decision maker. If that is impossible, try to obtain a commitment that the points of negotiation have been reviewed by the decision maker.Otherwise, you will wind up renegotiating the deal several times.

• Don't enter into negotiations without clear objectives, and always formulate alternative positions on each issue in advance. This will give you direction, and keep the process moving.

• Don't hesitate to be direct in asking for what you need or want, and, never take rejection personally! It's strictly business, so don't feel pressured into accepting conditions that are not beneficial.

• Don't stipulate a condition without a consequence. Evaluate the other side's options. If you can't think of a "reasonable" consequence, don't impose the condition! If you impose an unreasonable condition, you defeat the negotiation by placing the other party in an impossible position. "Reasonableness," however, is subject to negotiation. (Isn't this fun?!)

• Don't ignore prior agreements. If you do, you may appear arrogant and lose your credibility. That isn't to say you can't change your mind as the negotiation evolves, but if you do so arbitrarily or frivolously, you frustrate the other negotiator. The only valid time to change a prior agreement is when you are giving the other party a new concession in return for that change.

The anecdote *PRIDE and PRINCIPLE* at the beginning of this book helps to illustrate these points.

The best way to establish your "negotiating posture" is to **do your research!** This will do more to help you determine the priority of your bargaining points than you can imagine, yet is all too frequently overlooked.

Sources of research information are commercial brokers, property owners and managers, store owners and managers, newspaper classified ads, property signs, lenders, and attorneys. If you're a tenant, you might talk to the landlord's other tenants, or to the landlord's competitors, in order to determine the landlord's current state of affairs and bargaining position.

If you are a landlord, you should find a way to keep abreast of who's snooping around for space, why they are looking, and how financially qualified they are. Business journals often provide current and insightful profiles of companies in the area. They also often rely on commercial real estate brokers as information sources.

 Critical items of research information for both tenants and landlords include:

- base rental rates
- levels of percentage rents (minimum, maximum, average)
- the frequency and magnitude of rent increases
- the length of leases being signed
- inducements being offered by landlords
- concessions being made by tenants
- the terms of renegotiations
- current and projected vacancy rates

In addition, it is wise to find out who is moving in, and who is moving out! Who is building? How long has the market been in its present condition, and what is the near-term outlook — overall and for the specific neighborhood? This will determine the reasonableness of demands for concessions, or the need for offering incentives (depending on which side of the table you're on).

Typical incentives include the following (also see Exhibit E):

- Extra tenant improvement (remodeling) dollars.
- Assumption of a tenant's existing lease obligations (taking over a short term, low cost lease, as the tenant signs a higher cost, longer term lease).
- Rent concessions (free rent, structured rent, etc.).
- Paying tenant's moving costs.
- Combinations of the above.

Successful negotiations require anticipation of the other party's needs, that is, *discovering the "hidden agenda."* Effective research goes a long way towards enabling you to determine what might be important to the other party. Also, the extent to which you do not know the laws and market practices in an area dictates the extent to which legal and brokerage counsel are needed.

Having completed your research, you are ready to communicate your initial proposal to the other party. You should be aware of the fact that **either the landlord or the tenant can institute negotiations.** As the leasing agent for the owner of a major development project, I once badgered an office supply company for months, hoping to convince them to lease space at a newly created intersection. When they finally accepted our offer, it turned out to be the best store in their chain!

After preliminary discussions produce fundamental accord on the major issues, the tenant usually submits an "Offer to Lease" (see Exhibit B) to the landlord, who incorporates the provisions of the offer (if acceptable) into *his* "standard form lease," which is then submitted to the tenant for review and signature. Typically, the landlord executes (signs) the lease *after the tenant* to eliminate the possibility of subsequent changes.

TIMING

It's been said before, and it's true. Timing is everything! With leasing, as with everything else, you have to be in the right place at the right time. Sometimes it's mere chance that puts you there. But most of the time it's research and planning.

Real estate markets are cyclical, on both the "macro" and "micro" levels. "Macro" refers to the economy as a whole, "micro" to a specific location. Developers develop when lenders lend. Discussion of the economic conditions that induce lenders to make real estate loans could fill a whole book. For now, we'll take it as a fact that cycles do occur, and limit this discussion to their characteristics, and how they affect lease negotiations.

Like all cycles, real estate cycles have three phases; beginning, peak, and end. If you want to know exactly where the market is at any point in time, listen to business news on television and read newspapers. The market is always one phase ahead of where the media reports it to be! The news media is not in the "prognostication" business. They merely endeavor to make the general public aware of a phase after it has been around for a while. That's when it becomes "news"! And I'm not picking on the media; it's just the nature of their business.

To identify which phase the cycle is in, it is necessary to understand the characteristics of each phase, as follows:

- **BEGINNING PHASE**

  There is a lot of pent-up demand. Business has been slow. Companies that have been consolidating are planning growth strategies. Vacancy rates and inventory levels are relatively low and stable. Interest rates have been steady, and are also relatively low. Optimism is increasing in the community. Prices are steady. Tenants begin to enter the market. Rumors of new deals spread like wildfire. The natives are restless!

- **PEAK PHASE:**

  The initial burst of leasing activity has absorbed most of the inventory existing at the start. Newspapers begin to report about the deals that were made. If the perceived market demand is for an additional one million square feet of space, twenty-five local developers driven by basic greed are racing to build that same one million square feet, or parts of it! Land deals are made like crazy. Developers swarm lenders with loan proposals. Lenders start making loans like crazy. Buildings spring up everywhere, overnight! It looks like a "feeding frenzy"!

- **END PHASE:**

  By now, the news media is reporting regularly on all the land deals that were made. Even bank economists feel safe in predicting a strong market. Construction continues, but at a somewhat less-frantic pace because there aren't as many tenants showing up as there used to be. People begin talking about a slowdown (but not very loud; and, never in front of the boss!). Prices soften in response to decreased demand. At this point, nearly all twenty-five million square feet of space needed to satisfy that one million square feet of *demand* has been built or planned. Fewer concrete trucks are seen on the road. Landlords become a lot easier to deal with. (When will they learn?)

As you can see from this less-than-scientific portrayal of the real estate cycle, the point at which negotiations are started can make a huge difference on their outcome. It should be obvious that the tenant's likelihood of making a "fat" deal is good at the beginning of a cycle, and best at the end. The developer needs to shoot for the peak to do best.

In the beginning phase, landlords have more money available for making concessions to prospective tenants, since the projects are just getting under way. However, because times are good and the outlook rosy, landlords are reluctant to make concessions. As the market reaches its peak, competition forces ever-increasing concessions. Finally, in the end the landlord's ability to make concessions is weakest *at the time when tenants need them most* because business conditions are generally weakening. Developers have exhausted their resources, and owners of existing properties have trouble refinancing to provide tenant improvements because of sagging rents (due to overbuilding) and a dimming economic outlook. All of which hastens "the end."

Unfortunately, the end of a real estate cycle usually coincides with, or is precipitated by, an economic recession. For this reason, the length and severity of downturns is difficult to predict. It depends on how deep the recession is, and how badly over-built the market was. Remember, developers or tenants who base their timing strategy on media or bank reports are probably going to be a phase behind. This is the "macro" side of the cycle. Now let's look at the "micro" side.

Real estate is a "local" business. One region of the country, or one state in the region, or one city in the state, or one neighborhood in the city can easily be doing better or worse than others, at the same point in time. It depends on the diversity of industries, and the specific companies located in a market area. Areas with a highly diversified economy can often weather an "economic storm" with relatively little damage, while a single-industry or single-company town can be devastated by a slowdown.

To confirm this, look at the heavy geographic concentrations of properties owned by the Resolution Trust Corporation (RTC). In the 1980's, the "sunbelt" and the "oil belt" regions were booming while the "rust belt" region of the midwest languished. Now, properties in Texas, California, and Colorado predominate the RTC's portfolio. Surprise!

In "Silicon Valley" in the late 1980's, most of the area was disgustingly overbuilt. Developers couldn't give buildings away. The media coined a new phrase — "see-through buildings" — to describe the incredible vacancy problem in the area. "Free rent" for one to two years on a five year lease was the order of the day. Yet the city of Cupertino, California, was booming! The reason? Apple Computer was world-headquartered there, and Apple was on a roll. When Apple's market got a worm in it, Cupertino's absorption was drastically cut back—right along with the general rent level!

This, then, is the "micro" side of the cycle. The trick to profitable real estate leasing is to be in the right place at the right time. Because real estate is immoveable, and illiquid in a "down market," those with the best "local knowledge," who research and plan the timing of their negotiations, have the best "luck" and make the best deals.

CONCLUSION:

Preliminary negotiations are most often restricted to "hard-money" issues, which are discussed in the next section. In these negotiations, landlords and leasing agents should be careful to emphasize the positive aspects of a tenant's offer. If you are a landlord, don't just tell tenants what is wrong with their offer. Tell them *why* the offer is inadequate, and suggest alternatives. Maybe the tenant can modify its position; maybe not. But at least you will know that your position is clear. Sounds basic, I know. But you would be surprised at how many times I have had offers rejected with little or no explanation. It's simply counter-productive and rude!

To summarize, these are the steps in the tenant's leasing process:

1. The need arises for space
2. A general location is selected
3. The real estate market is researched
4. A space is selected
5. Preliminary negotiations are conducted
6. An offer to lease is submitted, usually by the tenant
7. The terms of the lease offer are negotiated
8. The lease is drafted, usually by the landlord
9. The lease is reviewed by the parties
10. The objectionable terms are renegotiated & amended
11. The lease is signed (or the tenant starts over!)

HOW TO "READ" THE LEASE

The first commercial lease ever negotiated was probably a simple thing done with a handshake on a couple of business points (I don't know this for sure, but it seems logical to me). Then some landlords and tenants started trying to take advantage of one another. So the lease had to be written down, had to cover a few more points and become much more precise. But business people are competitive types, so they began to find ways to circumvent some of those written-down provisions, which caused lawyers to get excited and help pass some laws to control those contract-circumventing scoundrels. This complicated things immensely, and so the modern day lease evolved.

The point is, leases cover things that the parties **want** to happen, or want to **prevent** from happening, or that **might** happen, based on their experience of what has *already* happened.

Since the commercial lease is a legal document designed to deal with all these things, it is full of facts and figures—no color, no humor. In a word—BORING!!

The trick to *understanding* the lease is to make "reading it" bearable. The trick to *that* is to breath some life into the review process. The way to do *that* is to read the lease with a purpose. And to do that you must learn to *read the lease in the context of your deal.* After all, your lease *defines* your deal. To review the lease in the "context of your deal," as you read each clause, ask yourself: "How could this provision (or this phrase) affect *my* business, given *my* particular circumstances?" This is the time to let your "what if" imagination run wild!

The "context of your deal" includes such considerations as:

- The lead time available for negotiations
- The importance of the facility to the parties.
- The *unique* requirements of both parties which the lease is supposed to address.
- The verbal agreement between the parties regarding major business points.

In other words, strive to *make the lease fit the situation* you are creating, instead of the other way around. The lease should *define* the bargain between the parties, not create a new one.

While most commercial leases contain the same basic provisions, there isn't much standard about the "standard form lease." It is, by and large, a misnomer. When you see the title at the top of a lease, it usually means it is the standard form for *that* particular landlord.

You should expect no particular ordering of the provisions in a lease document. Clauses relating to the same subject are usually scattered throughout the lease. I'm not sure if lawyers skip around like that on purpose, but they sure do confuse the issue by referring to paragraphs and exhibits and schedules all over the place!

But, if you manage to break it down and organize it, a commercial lease is fairly easy to understand. My "organizing" system, which is explained in the following paragraphs, shows you how to read all the related provisions *at one time*, so as not to lose your train of thought. That way, you can focus on one subject at a time as you read the various provisions. Assigning a *reading order* to your lease provisions is what I call "grouping". It is the most important thing you can learn about "how to read the lease."

To group provisions into a "reading order" you need to go through the table of contents of *your* lease (or *the lease itself*, if no table of contents is provided) and number each clause according to the "group numbers" in this book. Use the table of contents as your "guide" to the group numbers, plus, refer to "Exhibit A" as an example (right now!) to *see* what I mean. Now that you've seen it, here's the play by play.

Take a look at the table of contents of this book, noting the 18 groups of lease provisions. Starting with the Group 1 provisions (Demised Premises), search through *your* lease (or its table of contents) and mark every paragraph (or clause) related to "demised premises" with the number "1." Then find all the rent clauses and label them with a "2." Repeat this process for the rest of the applicable groups. Don't get all hung up on "which group" your clause falls into, it *may* fall into *two* different groups (see Exhibit A, paragraph #27). The main thing is that you get all your clauses numbered so you can *read all the related ones at one time*, and also know which group to refer to (in this book) for a clearer understanding of what those provisions mean.

OK, now that you've got that behind you, you're *almost* ready to start reading. I suggest that you begin by reviewing the "Landlord's Position" and "Tenant's Position" in Group 1. Then read all your clauses that are labeled with a 1. And most certainly, as the need arises, refer back to the specific provision in this book that relates to *your* lease provision. For instance, if you are reading a clause dealing with janitor service, you will want to specifically look at provision 9.05 in this book (Group 9, provision 5). Then make notes of any important points you need to remember (questions to ask, points to negotiate) and "check off" each provision after you read it (next to the group numbers you've assigned to each provision). Then repeat this process with all the provisions that fall into "Group 2," then "Group 3," etc. Got it? Great, you're now well on your way!

Here's another crucial point. In each group, all clauses are important, but *some clauses are more important than others.* In order to help you determine the relative importance of your lease clauses, each provision in the 18 groups of this book has been marked with "(H)" (Hard Money) or "(M)" (Marshmallow), and all the general or miscellaneous provisions have been gathered in Group 16. "Hard Money" clauses *definitely* affect the tenant financially. "Marshmallow" clauses only have *the potential* to affect the tenant financially (these are terms I invented, I think). Notice that I'm only speaking of how these clauses affect *tenants?* That's because, as I mentioned earlier, the *landlord* usually writes the lease, so very few clauses cost the landlord money. (The only time *a tenant* writes the lease is if it is someone like General Motors or McDonald's, whose "piles of gold" are bigger than everybody's, so they can make their own rules!)

Pay special attention to the "Hard Money" clauses. Then move on to the "Marshmallow" ones. After all, in negotiations, if you are unable to agree on the "hard money" issues, the "marshmallow" ones are not going to matter much, right?

Now you're ready to *actually read* the paragraphs, so you need to put yourself *in a negotiating state of mind.* Most people have never learned how to "read" a lease. Consequently, *their* negotiations take forever because they don't review the lease in an organized manner. One party might think the deal is just about done, while the other party starts reading some more provisions, and they wind up back at "square one" a dozen times! What a waste of time and energy!

To avoid this situation, you must devise a reading plan based on your own attention span. Decide how much time you have available to finish the review (days, weeks, months), then, break down the reading into segments that fit your ability to concentrate.

Stay on schedule. Don't procrastinate! But, if you find yourself daydreaming or mentally "drifting off," it's time to take a break.

As you read, underline or highlight profusely, and make cross-reference notes in the margins (e.g."See para. xx. . .", or "check with broker on. . ."). Also, if one provision refers to another (or to an exhibit), read the paragraphs and exhibits in the order in which they are referenced. Use a "post-it" note or paper clip to mark your place(s) if necessary as you skip around—and you *will* skip around! (refer again to Exhibit A) Don't fight it, just "go with the flow." If you try to start on the first page and read through to the last one, you won't know what you are signing! You will never remember what refers to what.

When you're all finished, review your notes and questions with your broker, attorney, or advisor, and have them presented to the other party. This can be done verbally in the preliminary stages, but should be formalized in an "Offer to Lease" (Exhibit B) as negotiations progress. If modifications to the "standard form lease" are extensive, they will normally be put together as "special provisions" in a separate exhibit at the end of the lease. I prefer this method, since it draws attention to all the changes in just one place, rather than having to search through the whole lease looking for modifications here and there.

Usually you will repeat this process several times until a document suitable for signing is developed. Depending on the size and complexity of the transaction, negotiations can take several weeks or even months. (My average gestation period per deal has been roughly 90 days.)

That's it! That's how you do it. Use this system and you will be surprised at how much easier it is to plow through a lease and put a deal together.

A FINAL WORD OF CAUTION!

"Referenced statutes" appear sporadically throughout most leases. They are easy to spot, since they always refer to a specific *code section and number*. Another type of clause to be alert for is the *waiver provision*, (e.g. "tenant hereby waives the right to. . .")

When you encounter them, write down the paragraph number and consult your attorney! Instruct your attorney to review these paragraphs specifically, and, to review them "in the context of your deal."

If you have no idea what the statutes or waivers mean, you are "flying blind"!!! If you sign a lease without a legal opinion on them, don't be surprised if down the road you hit a bump (or maybe a wall)! And if you are not an attorney, never attempt to explain them to someone else. "He who assumes, blunders!"

DISCLAIMER

The chapters that follow are *not* intended to constitute legal advice. They are supposed to provide the reader with a background for understanding common business points contained in most commercial leases. Remember, *always* look up unfamiliar terms in the Glossary or Index! My intention is to create a "guidebook" that will lead you through the lease negotiation process, making consultations with your attorney, as well as the actual negotiations themselves, much more productive.

We've all heard the expression "knowledge is power." In lease negotiations, if you know the reasons for each provision from *both* party's point of view, you possess negotiating power. Imparting that knowledge *to you* is the whole purpose of this book.

GROUP 1

DEMISED PREMISES

LANDLORD'S POSITION:

The landlord's objective is to convey occupancy to the tenant while maintaining the highest degree of control over the property.

TENANT'S POSITION:

The tenant wants to obtain the exact size of space needed, improved as closely as possible to accommodate its use, with the fewest restraints to overall operations.

The tenant almost always presumes the landlord has valid title to the property, and that the title is properly insured. However, the landlord's title policy often covers only the land cost. If a major commitment of time and money is contemplated, the tenant should investigate the cost and advantages of a leasehold owners policy, discussed in paragraph 18.01, Under "TITLE."

COMMONLY INCLUDED PROVISIONS:

1.01 DESCRIPTION (H)

The exact size, address, and list of tenant improvements existing, or, to be provided by the landlord, should be specified in detail. An exhibit and/or schedule should be used to outline the space on a site map and/or floor plan so the parties can visualize where the premises are located within the building or complex. Don't be afraid to insist that this be done accurately (a picture is worth a thousand words!).

Office buildings present a special situation. Unless the tenant occupies the whole floor, entries, hallways, stairways, elevators, and restroom areas are not directly rentable space. In order to allocate non-rentable space among all the tenants, a "load factor" is computed by dividing the net rentable area of the building by the gross floor area of the building, then subtracting the result from 100%.

It is normally applied in one of three ways. *First,* assuming the load-factor is 20%, a tenant wanting 10,000 square feet will actually be given 8,000 square feet of usable space.

100% - 20% "Load factor" = 80% × 10,000 sq. ft. = 8,000 sq. ft.

Or, with a load factor of 20% (or .2), the tenant would have to lease 12,500 square feet to have 10,000 square feet usable.

[Usable square feet, divided by (1 minus the load factor), equals square feet necessary to be leased].

$$10,000 \div (1-.2) = 12,500$$
or
$$10,000 \div .80 = 12,500$$

Alternatively, the base rent can be quoted with a load-factor added; for example, $2.00/Sf with a "load" of $.40/Sf ($2 x 20% = $.40). Obviously, the tenant must make it a point *during negotiations* to understand how non-rentable areas are allocated.

If *existing* interior improvements are extensive, they should be listed carefully on a separate schedule, and the condition of major components noted. This is important to ensure that the tenant gets what he bargained for at commencement, and could become important upon termination of the lease under the "surrender" provision (section 3.04).

If interior improvements are to be *constructed*, the regulations governing their construction are generally spelled out in the "Alterations & Repairs" provision (see Group 8). If this is the case, it should be stated in sufficient detail to clarify the understanding of the parties, including:

- the initial condition of the premises when delivered to the tenant
- which party is responsible for creating plans and specifications, and for obtaining building permits
- which party is responsible for paying for the work, and how much
- construction schedules, and penalties for delay.

1.02 POSSESSION/ACCEPTANCE OF DEFECTS (H)

The idea here is that the tenant has had an opportunity to inspect the premises and its major components, and, to have informed the landlord (in writing) of any deficiencies found during the inspection. The tenant's inspection should be thorough enough to determine if the building features are fundamentally suitable for the intended use.

For example, the load-bearing capacities of the floor and roof should be checked if unusually heavy equipment is to be installed, or an exceptional number of people will be occupying the space. I remember one instance where a night club owner leased a second floor space in an office building. Months later, after investing tens of thousands of dollars, he discovered that the floor could not withstand the weight he was planning to have inside. The structural modifications needed to correct the problem were both painfully costly and time-consuming.

A tenant in one of my buildings once placed a group of metal file drawer "safes" in the middle of their second floor space and filled them full of video tapes. After a while, the whole floor began to sag, and warped all the door jambs! Once again, the solution was expensive and time-consuming. Refer also to the discussion of "UTILITIES," Group 6. Never assume utility service or other features will be adequate. Investigate!

Once the tenant accepts the premises, the landlord has no responsibility to cure defects which surface subsequently, unless the parties have otherwise agreed in the lease. They will be deemed to have occurred during the tenant's occupancy, unless the tenant can prove the landlord intentionally and maliciously covered up the defects (that is, committed fraud).

Depending on the previous use, it may be wise to conduct a soils test and check for toxic contamination (see provision 18.01, "SOILS TEST"). Hazardous materials can remain undetected for years, even decades.

Asbestos and "PCB" (which is commonly used in electrical transformers) are the most common offenders. Concrete walls and floors have been removed and hauled to certified toxic-waste disposal sites during the clean-up of transformer explosions! The use of storage tanks, solvents or motor oil should always be suspected of contamination and checked thoroughly before signing a lease.

Toxic contamination is a serious environmental problem gaining momentum as a legal and financial issue. Landlords and tenants should deal with it carefully. I believe the subject deserves its own provision in the standard form lease, although the issue is seldom even specifically mentioned!

1.03 NO LIGHT OR AIR EASEMENT (M)

I once heard a story about an Atlantic City developer who bought the rights to an air easement and built a multi-million dollar casino over an existing residence because the owner refused to sell the house. That's why landlord's put this provision in their lease. The value of land includes the rights to use, and sell, air space. This includes the right to demolish a building and construct a higher one, with obvious rent advantages.

Suppose a landlord plans to seek a change to the height limit restricting his property. He does not want to be prohibited from adding more stories to the building because the tenant has put a lounge or a heliport on the roof-top. And if a landlord owns the adjoining lot, he does not want to be precluded from building on it just because his existing tenant's view might be impeded.

1.04 ALARM SYSTEM (H)

This provision can entail anything from the requirement for a tenant to install a simple alarm system within the premises, to the landlord's right to include security guards and parking attendants as common area expenses.

The degree of complexity and cost to the tenant depends on the situation. Securing space in a shopping mall will likely be a bit more involved than securing a small machine shop space in an industrial building.

Some tenants might want to install extremely elaborate security systems involving structural elements (e.g., heating and ventilating ducts), which will usually require the landlord's prior written approval.

1.05 RULES & REGULATIONS—EXHIBIT "X" (M)

Most leases contain a group of provisions designed to regulate the daily behavior of tenants in the building or complex. Often, these are contained in an exhibit which can be readily modified to fit the specific and unique needs of the property.

Common inclusions are parking rules, garbage and trash collection policies, use of roof areas, outside storage, pest control, control of noise and odors, recreational vehicle storage, on-site traffic regulations, use of locks in and around the premises, restrictions on hours of service in lobbies, delivery areas, and other rules for the common good of the building.

Tenants should review these rules in the context of their individual situation. Make sure no provisions interfere directly with your ability to function, or inflict undue costs of compliance.

1.06 ACCESS OF LANDLORD TO PREMISES (M)

To make routine repairs, major renovations, or in case of an emergency, the landlord sometimes needs access to the tenant's premises. Such work can be inconsequential, or it could involve significant construction or emergency repairs. The issues are:

- the nature and timing of the landlord's notice to the tenant

- precautions required to be taken by the landlord prior to commencing work

- placing liability for damage and injury.

Many leases allow the landlord to keep a pass key or master key. If this poses a unique security problem for the tenant due to the sensitivity of information, value of inventory items, or for some other reason, it should be addressed specifically in this clause.

GROUP 2

RENT

LANDLORD'S POSITION:

More is better! For the landlord, utopia is the ability to receive an infinite amount of rent while providing the tenant absolutely nothing.

TENANT'S POSITION:

For tenants, utopia is exactly the opposite of the landlord's. Somewhere in between is where deals are made.

COMMONLY INCLUDED PROVISIONS:

2.01 TIME AND PLACE OF PAYMENT (H)

This basic provision spells out the day of the month on which rent becomes due, where it is to be paid, and the manner of payment -- normally U.S. Dollars (no acorns or elephants, please).

2.02 MINIMUM FIXED RENT (H)

For new developments, landlords prepare a proforma income and cost statement which becomes the basis of their financing. (I finally developed a software package called "The Real Estate Development System" to take the drudgery out of doing these projections.) During the lease-up period, all negotiations are geared toward achieving those rent projections. The extent to which contract rents fall short of the proforma rents determines the amount of additional cash needed to close the gap between total costs and the loan. Generally speaking, the higher the rent, the higher the loan amount.

As a result, heated debates often arise between tenants and landlords over the last dime of rent! "It's only a dime, what difference can it make?" For the tenant, a dime a square foot on 20,000 sq. ft. amounts to $2,000 per month, $24,000 per year, and $120,000 total over a 5-year term. I'll take it...

But, watch the impact of that dime on the landlord. If the $24,000 is "net" rent (see Group 9), and the "cap rate" for valuation of the property is 10%, that rent is worth $240,000 in added market value! If the lender is requiring a "debt coverage ratio" of 1.25 times, the dime is worth roughly $182,000 in additional financing, presuming a 30-year loan at 10% per year.

Annual net rent	$24,000
Divided by debt svc. cvg.	1.25
yields	
Avail. for debt pmts.	19,200
Divided by Loan constant (30yr @ 10%)	.1053
Loan amount	$182,336

The point is, expect the developer of a new building to watch his pennies. They mean loan dollars, and lots of them!

Now if this were an existing building and the landlord was *refinancing* it, that $182,000 would be "tax free" (until disposition of the property), because financing proceeds are not taxable. I'll take that, too!

Owners of existing buildings usually price their space near prevailing market levels for new space, and depending on the terms of their financing, have a bit more flexibility in establishing rents.

2.03 ADDITIONAL RENT (H)

This provision usually stipulates the tenant's duty to pay excise taxes levied on rent, a pro-rata share of property taxes and common area expenses, and a pro-rata share of current or future assessments on the property.

It's more like a "warning," since these items are usually covered in detail elsewhere in the lease.

2.04 COMMENCEMENT OF RENT (H)

This can be either very simple or very complicated. If the tenant takes the premises in their existing condition, no problem. Pick a date; rent starts...BUT,

If interior improvements need to be constructed or modified, it is a whole different story. The landlord may be anxious to collect the rent as early as possible, but **the tenant needs time for build-out**. Plans must be drawn and submitted to the landlord (the tenant will want to obligate the landlord to use diligence in reviewing the plans). Then the plans must be submitted to the proper governmental agencies for their approval and building permits. Next, a construction contract must be negotiated and closed. Finally, the *actual construction* requires even *more* time before the tenant can move in.

If the tenant requires a building permit, a zoning variance, a liquor license, or other approvals, **a reasonable time period should be allowed to complete the governmental process before rent starts.** Each of these processes can take months to complete, but some can be done concurrently. For planning purposes during negotiations, contact the city, county, state, and federal agencies to learn how their approval processes work, and to establish time estimates for each step required. Individual circumstances of the parties, and of the government agencies involved, will dictate the solution to the commencement date problem. But these are the issues at hand.

2.05 EXPENDITURES BY LANDLORD (M)

This is kind of a "catch-all" provision which states that if the tenant does not do or pay for something and the landlord thinks it is important, the landlord can do or pay for it and charge the tenant for costs incurred.

Sounds fair, but the landlord should be required to notify the tenant first, and then be restricted to charging reasonable (market) prices.

GROUP 3

TERM

LANDLORD'S POSITION:

Generally, longer is better. Longer terms reduce the landlord's need to advertise for prospective tenants, negotiate leases, and renovate the property. Also, lenders prefer long term leases because of the increased assurance of the landlord's income stream for making mortgage payments.

TENANT'S POSITION:

The length of the term should fit individual requirements. Shorter terms reduce exposure if business plans fail or change, but longer terms usually result in a more favorable rent schedule because landlords prefer them,and, longer terms give the landlord more room to maneuver (see Exhibit E).

COMMONLY INCLUDED PROVISIONS:

3.01 TERM DEFINED (H)

Most leases have a "commencement date" and a "termination date" specifically defined. As stated above, these dates are completely subject to negotiation. Retailers, for example, might insist on ending the lease in January or February, allowing for completion of the Christmas season; accountants might insist on a date after April 15!

I'm afraid the Pharaoh will insist on a rather long lease. . .

3.02 EARLY ACCESS / EARLY OCCUPANCY (H)

This provision allows the tenant to use and occupy the premises subject to all the terms and conditions of the lease, except for the payment of rent. There are two principal reasons for it. First, the tenant needs time to construct interior improvements and/or install trade fixtures. Second, the landlord offers a period of "free rent" as an inducement to obtain a tenant. (See Exhibit E).

3.03 OPTION TO EXTEND (H)

Tenants love them. Most landlords don't. An option to renew gives the tenant effective control of the premises without having to pay for it! If the landlord has the opportunity to transact an extremely favorable lease, the option holder must first be dealt with. In addition, since nobody knows what market conditions will be upon lease expiration, establishing rent for the renewal period is always a challenge.

On the other hand, if the tenant has made a sizable investment over time in physical improvements, or, in advertising and promoting the location, or both, it behooves the tenant to secure its longevity with an option provision. This is especially true if the lease contains a "no obligation to renew" clause (see provision 11.05).

One solution is to simply agree to set the renewal period rent at "market" rates. Another is to set a "fixed amount" for the renewal period. This usually works if the market is stable, and the initial term is not too long. Another way is to adjust the option rent by a "fixed percentage" for each year of the initial term, where the percentage used is the result of the parties' mutual agreement on the anticipated inflation rate during the initial term.

A common, and much more complicated way to determine option period rent, is the "consumer price index (CPI) adjustment" method. This one was probably invented by lawyers. It usually takes a page or two of precise language to define how the rent will be computed. Here's how it works. . .

First, the "index" to be used is defined, which most often is the CPI for the nearest major metropolitan area to the property. Next, the "base year" is defined, usually as the beginning of the first year of the initial term. Then, a "quotient" is established by dividing the renewal year index by the base year index. Finally, the rent at the expiration date of the initial term is multiplied by the quotient to obtain the renewal period rent. The frequency of applying the formula (which option years to adjust) must also be negotiated (1st, 3rd, 5th, etc).

This method produces a precise formula, but unfortunately does not always produce a workable result. The problem is that real estate markets don't always move in step with inflation. They are much more influenced by "supply and demand." If a market develops an extremely low vacancy rate during a period of low inflation, market rents are likely to be much higher than inflation-adjusted rents. Of course, the reverse is also true.

For example, during the Carter administration recession of the early 80's, double-digit inflation rates drove the CPI's through the roof. I found myself continually renegotiating with tenants who refused to pay lofty rent increases computed under CPI formulas when, at that time, vacancy rates were setting peak records and pushing rent levels down through the floor! For this reason, CPI adjustment clauses often contain a "minimum" rent, and, a "lid" on the percentage increase. So, you ask, "Why bother with all this CPI exercise"? Good point.

That's why, instead of CPI computed increases, I like "fixed amount" or "fixed percentage" options for short term leases (up to 3 years), and "market" options for long term leases.

Additionally, if a landlord's ground lease includes minimum rent increases, or if his loan has interest rate escalation provisions, the tenant's rent increases will have to keep "in sync" with the landlord's rent increases in order to preserve the landlord's cash flow. Ultimately, the best method for setting option rents is the one that results in a deal!

Some leases contain an "impasse provision." If the parties cannot agree on the amount of rent, the impasse provision establishes a procedure for selecting three experienced appraisers. If they arrive at a "consensus," the agreed-upon amount is used; otherwise, the average of the three becomes the option period rent. However, if the low and high rents deviate from the average by a significant percentage (e.g., 10 to 15), the middle rent is used. Any deficit between the rent the tenant was paying during the appraisal process and the new rent becomes due immediately, usually with interest.

3.04 SURRENDER-INSPECTION & CONDITION (M)

When a tenant moves out, the landlord has to re-lease the property. The interior improvements will be an asset or a liability to the building depending on their nature. If they are of the "cookie-cutter" variety, they can readily be used by a wide range of tenants. If they are highly customized, they probably will be considered a detriment. The surrender provision gives the landlord the option to keep the improvements intact, or to require the tenant to remove them.

Most leases require the premises to be in "broom clean condition, normal wear and tear excepted." If the interiors are provided by the landlord, and it is likely that they will remain, a detailed list of improvements and their original condition should be made at the outset. The surrender clause should require an inspection and approval by both parties immediately upon expiration of the lease. Moreover, where caustic chemicals are used by the tenant, the landlord should consider requiring a soils test (see provision 18.01).

3.05 SURRENDER-HOLDING OVER   (M)

If a new lease or an extension of the current lease has not been negotiated by the time the lease term expires, the tenant is said to be "holding over." As an inducement to the tenant to come to an agreement with the landlord, the holding over clause imposes a penalty in the form of a rent premium on the tenant. Usually it is 150% to 200% of the last applicable rent under the original lease. This will induce most tenants to come to terms with their landlord!

GROUP 4

USE

LANDLORD'S POSITION:

The landlord, as owner, is responsible for the general well-being of the occupants. Consequently, it behooves him to control what happens on the property. The use clause is the tool available for this purpose.

TENANT'S POSITION:

The tenant wants to negotiate the broadest definition for the operation of its business within the premises, and perhaps preclude the landlord from renting to competitors.

COMMONLY INCLUDED PROVISIONS:

4.01   DEFINITION OF USE   (H)

To be effective, the use clause must state the specific purpose for which the premises are leased, and prohibit all other uses. Using the word "may" when defining the use can be dangerous, since it implies that the tenant has an option, but is not obligated, to undertake a certain use. The phrase "shall be used for" works much better.

In an office or industrial building, the use clause is primarily intended to ensure that uses are restricted to functions for which the building was structurally designed, and that they conform to zoning ordinances. In retail centers, negotiating the use clause is far more exciting.

If the center contains department stores or supermarkets, *their* leases are signed first, then those for the "in-line" or satellite stores. In this scenario, "use clause" negotiations can get *very specific,* even down to defining the number of square feet allocated to various types of products.

Sometimes the tenant negotiates a non-competition clause which prohibits the landlord from leasing to other tenants engaged in the same business. It then becomes mandatory for the landlord to strictly prohibit that use in other tenants' leases, or to screen out certain types of tenants entirely.

4.02 COMPLIANCE WITH LAWS & ORDINANCES (H)

The important thing for the tenant is that its intended use complies with the zoning ordinances and building codes for the property. There's nothing like having a fire marshall close down your operation after you've made a costly investment in the facility. Sometimes the tenant will settle for the insertion of language which states that the landlord "guarantees the building to be suitable for the intended use." But if the landlord has not done his homework, this is no guarantee at all, and there could still be a lot of trouble looming on the horizon.

On the other hand, the landlord will insist that he be indemnified against a tenant's violation of such ordinances after possession is conveyed. This can be especially important where the possibility of toxic contamination exists (refer to provision 18.01).

4.03 ANNOYING OR INJURIOUS CONDUCT (M)

The landlord needs to be assured that no illegal uses occur which would cause problems with the mortgage loan, or with another tenant's "quiet enjoyment." This provision prohibits the tenant from using the property for illegal purposes, or for uses that violate zoning laws. It also prohibits uses which will cause damage to the property, or become a nuisance to other tenants.

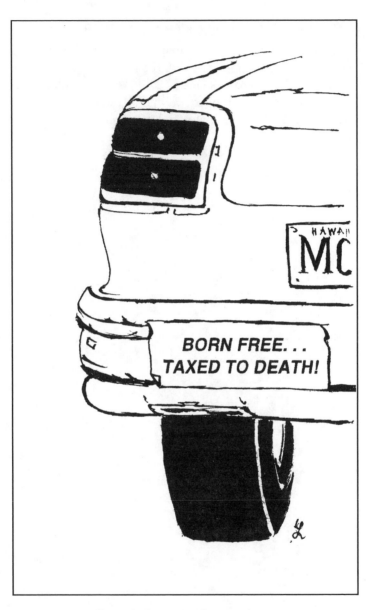

There's no end to taxes. . .

GROUP 5

TAXES

LANDLORD'S POSITION:

There's no end to taxes—old or new! Legislators, regulators, and bureaucrats search eternally for new and more devious ways to tax, assess, license, impose fees, and otherwise reach into our pocket books. Needless to say, the landlord wants to be protected from both known and *potential* taxation which could destroy the economics of the deal.

TENANT'S POSITION:

Tenant's don't like taxes either. They, too, have economics. But, by and large, they must succumb to the "Gold Rule". . . (you *do* have this rule committed to memory now, don't you?).

COMMONLY INCLUDED PROVISIONS:

5.01 BASIS FOR DETERMINATION (H)

The tenant is going to be charged for taxes and assessments. This clause sets forth which taxes are included as the tenant's responsibility. Most common are real estate taxes as assessed by the city or county, and assessment bond payments charged to the tax bill (see provision 5.08).

5.02 PRO-RATA SHARE (H)

When the demised premises are part of a larger building or complex of buildings, it becomes necessary to apportion each tenant's share of the costs of operating the property. Often, the computation of pro-rata share for taxes is used for all other common area (Group 8) charges as well, so it pays both parties to scrutinize the computation. Typically, these costs are pro-rated based on the tenant's percentage of the total floor area leasable in the building or complex.

The complexity of the definition of floor area depends on whether the premises are part of another building, or complex, or resort. This definition should be reviewed carefully, and compared to site and/or floor plans provided in the exhibits to the lease. At a minimum, be sure the total rentable square footage of the property is stated in the lease, and that the square footage or dimensions of the premises are shown on an exhibit.

Most often, the dimensions are measured from the "center-of-wall to the center-of-wall." As an example, if the walls are six inches thick, then 3 inches would be added to all four sides of the between-the-wall measurements, or 6 inches to each dimension. For this reason, it is common to see the words "hereby acknowledged to be (so many) square feet" describing the size of the leased premises.

The tenant's pro-rata share is computed by dividing the floor area (square feet) in the *demised* (leased) premises by the *total* floor area in the building or complex.

5.03 TAXES ON TENANT'S PROPERTY (H)

Many municipalities impose a personal property tax on non-real estate assets. These taxes are the tenant's responsibility, and the lease declares it a default if the tenant somehow allows such taxes to become a lien on the landlord's property.

5.04 GROSS INCOME TAX (M)

Some states, Hawaii being one, impose a "General Excise Tax," which taxes *everything* that changes hands — including rents! Most landlords under commercial leases charge tenants the amount of such tax as extra rent. Moreover, this provision sometimes states that if there exists an "income" tax on the tenant's business profits, the landlord refuses to pay it for the tenant. Talk about paranoid! But I guess you can't be too careful!

5.05 CONVEYANCE TAXES (H)

Here again, some jurisdictions have found a way to charge people for "conveying" leased premises. Of course, the tenant gets to pay this tax, too.

5.06 OTHER TAXES (M)

In case some tax laws pass that the landlord didn't think of, this provision says the tenant will pay those taxes too. The tenant can object, but the landlord can refuse to sign the lease. Again, the "Gold Rule" reigns...

5.07 RIGHT TO CONTEST TAXES (M)

Tax rates are usually determined by dividing the municipality's budget by the total assessed valuation of all property on its tax roll. Politicians, economics, physical disasters, and tax assessors all being what they are, can sometimes cause wild fluctuations in tax bills from one year to the next. (Remember "Proposition 13" in California?!)

If the tenant is obligated to pay the taxes, this provision conveys to the tenant the right to contest the amount of taxes levied on the property—*after* having paid the tax bill. In addition, which party will be responsible for paying the legal and other costs of the contest will be stated in the lease. (Guess who!)

5.08 ASSESSMENTS (M)

In many municipalities, certain public services and infrastructure elements are financed with "assessment bonds." Schools, streets, sanitary and storm sewer systems, electrical service, police and fire stations, libraries, etc. are sometimes financed by assessment bonds which are added to property owners' tax bills on a pro-rata basis throughout the subdivision.

In accordance with the "Gold Rule," these costs are passed on to the tenant.

GROUP 6

UTILITIES

LANDLORD'S POSITION:

Three things are important to the landlord regarding utilities: making sure they exist, making sure they are adequate, and making sure someone else pays for them.

TENANT'S POSITION:

To the tenant also, three things are important regarding utilities: where they are located, their adequacy for the intended use, and how much it costs to bring them into the premises and use them.

COMMONLY INCLUDED PROVISIONS:

6.01 PAYMENT OF CHARGES (H)

In a "net" lease (see Group 9), the tenant directly pays the entire cost of all utilities. The issue of which party pays for bringing the utilities to the premises, and for maintaining their physical condition, is subject to negotiation. Normally, the landlord will supply utility service "to" the premises, and the tenant is responsible for "distribution" and maintenance inside.

In a "gross" lease, or, where utilities are not separately metered (either because the utility company refused to do so, or the landlord wanted to reduce construction costs), the landlord pays the bills, then invoices the tenant(s), sometimes adding a service charge. In this case, a "building usage standard" is set by the landlord, and restrictions included in the lease on the permitted types of fixtures and equipment. This allows excessive users to be charged a premium. Obviously, it's a good idea for the tenant to evaluate the "standard" during negotiations.

Both parties should investigate the availability and adequacy for the intended use of gas, electricity, water, sewer, and telephone. Unavailable or inadequate utility service can be costly to rectify, very time-consuming, and depending upon what representations were made, lead you right to the courtroom!

Just because one building in a complex, or one space in a building, has gas service doesn't necessarily mean others will. The presence of water faucets is no guarantee that the water main is adequate to supply a given tenant's needs. And don't assume there will be enough phone lines available in any given building to satisfy your requirements if you plan to install a lot of faxes, phones, and modem lines! Check with "Ma Bell" *before* signing the lease.

6.02 COOLING TOWER CHARGES (H)

Some complexes use a water cooling tower to operate air conditioning equipment. In this case, tenant's are billed pro-rata for their usage of "ton-hours." "What are *those*," you ask?

Well, ton-hours are calculated by multiplying the tenant's business hours during a billing period by the *tonnage* of the tenant's air conditioning equipment (tonnage is simply a measurement of the cooling tower's ability to cool water. The pro-rata share then, is the tenant's ton-hours divided by the total ton-hours produced by the cooling tower. I just *knew* you would want to know this.

If you are not clear as to how the costs of operation, and how the "total ton-hours produced" are determined, you ought to find out before signing the lease so you can estimate your share and include it in your "Occupancy Cost Analysis" (Exhibit F).

Where a conventional central air-conditioning system is used, or roof-mounted "package" units are installed, most landlords will choose to provide a master service contract to ensure that the equipment is properly maintained. In this case, a pro-rata or per-unit charge is billed to each tenant. Be sure the lease is clear about who does the maintenance and how the cost is apportioned, so it can be included in the tenant's "Occupancy Cost Analysis" (Exhibit F).

6.03 NON-LIABILITY FOR INTERRUPTION (M)

Unless caused by malice or the willful neglect of the landlord, there usually is no rent abatement for interruption of utility service. It's kind of like the situation when your cable television goes out in the middle of the Super Bowl!

The tenant might try to insert a provision requiring the landlord to use diligence in attempting to have service restored, or to provide alternate sources (such as installing a temporary generator) if normal service cannot be resumed within a reasonable period of time. But don't expect the landlord to cave in easily on this point unless the tenant is in an extremely strong negotiating position.

GROUP 7

SECURITY DEPOSIT

LANDLORD'S POSITION:

The security deposit is the landlord's "performance insurance." It should relate to the size of the landlord's investment, the monthly rent, the presumed risk of damage from the tenant's use, or the risk of toxic contamination of the premises. One month's rent is common, but not necessarily appropriate. The amount ought to be significant enough that the tenant wants it back!

TENANT'S POSITION:

It's pretty hard to get around this one. About the only way to avoid putting up a security deposit is to push your financial weight around. According to Fortune Magazine, General Motors is the largest public industrial corporation in the world. They probably don't pay security deposits. On the other hand, "Louie & Chewey" can always count on paying one.

Some potential *alternative* or even *additional* security deposits (for tenants who are short on capital or financial stability) are: a personal guarantee backed by substantial net worth, hypothecation of marketable securities, posting a surety bond, or providing the landlord a letter of credit.

COMMONLY INCLUDED PROVISIONS:

7.01 USE AND RETURN (H)

The security deposit is usually paid when the lease is signed. Once in a while it is paid in installments over several months. The landlord holds it, most often without paying interest, until the lease expires to insure the tenant's performance of all the covenants in the lease. Most "standard form" leases fail to define in detail the reasons for which the deposit will be withheld or reduced, but it's a good idea to list specific acts of default. Rest assured that if you are in a dispute with the landlord at the time the lease expires, you're not about to see your security deposit until it is resolved.

If any portion of the deposit is used by the landlord to cure a default, the tenant must restore it to the original amount, pronto (often within 5 days). The lease should state when the deposit is to be returned to the tenant (30 days after expiration is common), and any specific reasons for which a portion will be kept by the landlord. It's a good idea to tie this point to the "SURRENDER—CONDITION AND INSPECTION" clause (provision 3.04).

The lease should clearly state that the deposit will be held in trust for the tenant and will not be used to pay the last month's rent. Otherwise, it becomes taxable to the landlord upon receipt!

7.02 APPLICATION IN CASE OF BANKRUPTCY (M)

Bankruptcy is used to protect a debtor from its creditors. Under the various bankruptcy law "chapters," a debtor's assets will be either "liquidated" or "reorganized." Either way, the creditors usually wind up with a fraction of what they are owed.

Should the tenant file bankruptcy proceedings, this provision affords the landlord the protection of applying the security deposit *first* to any amounts owed prior to the filing, and any balance to amounts owed *afterwards*.

7.03 TRANSFER OF SECURITY (M)

The sale or transfer of the landlord's interest in the property requires the transfer of the tenant's security deposit to the new owner, which terminates the landlord's responsibility for it.

7.04 UCC1 FINANCING STATEMENT (M)

A *Uniform Commercial Code Financing Statement* serves a similar purpose for personal property as a mortgage or a trust deed does for real estate. It "evidences" a security interest in the property. To secure their lease obligations, some tenants are required by the landlord to place a "UCC1" on their furniture, trade fixtures, and tenant improvements as an addition to the security deposit. This is an effective tool for a financially weak tenant to use as an inducement, but I have found it to be an easy clause for a strong tenant to have deleted from the lease.

Notes

GROUP 8

ALTERATIONS & REPAIRS

LANDLORD'S POSITION:

Alterations are modifications to the structural elements of a building. Repairs deal with the maintenance of the premises that existed at the time of acceptance. Both are very important because they can be extremely costly. The crucial point for the landlord is to maintain control over whatever work takes place on the property by retaining the right to review and approve plans prior to commencement of any construction. The review process also gives the landlord enough time to post a "notice of non-responsibility" (for payments) on the jobsite.

Unless it is a single-tenant net lease, the landlord usually maintains responsibility for structural alterations so as to preserve the integrity of the building. Repairs are controlled to prevent bizarre construction within the premises, and to assure adherence to building codes and other local ordinances. Properly constructed improvements can vastly increase the value of the building, and vice versa. It is not uncommon for interior improvements to cost far more than the building shell.

TENANT'S POSITION:

Two points should be covered by the tenant. First, structural repairs should be done so as to minimize inconvenience to employees, customers and vendors, and, commenced only after proper notice whenever possible. Second, structural alterations should not affect entrances, stairways, dimensions and other building features which materially diminish the utility of the premises for the tenant without some form of consideration.

COMMONLY INCLUDED PROVISIONS:

8.01   STRUCTURAL REPAIRS BY LANDLORD   (M)

During the lease term, if structural repairs become necessary, the tenant is required to notify the landlord in writing of the need for such repairs. The landlord is required to act expeditiously to make needed repairs, and to bear their cost. However, the clause usually provides that if the repairs are the result of the tenant's malicious, careless, or neglectful behavior, the tenant will pay the cost.

"Structural elements" should be defined, and should specifically include: the exterior walls; the exterior roof; the interior roof structure or system; plumbing to the building; water, gas, electrical, and telephone service to the building; the sprinkler system to the building; and the common area.

If the building has elevators, escalators, loading docks, sump pumps, or a central heating and air conditioning system, the lease should state clearly the extent of the landlord's responsibility for their maintenance and repair.

So that there is no misunderstanding, check the "Common Area" (Group 9) provisions carefully for language regarding who pays for these repairs! Many leases provide for the landlord to "operate and maintain" the common elements of the building or complex, and to be reimbursed for such common area maintenance costs. No problem, so long as the basic rent is properly negotiated on a "gross" or a "net" basis (see Group 9). Close scrutiny will avert costly "oh, by the way" expenses down the road. Remember, the "Gold Rule" is always in effect.

8.02 TENANT'S CONSTRUCTION OBLIGATIONS (H)

Rarely can a tenant move into a building without needing some fixturing or modifications to customize it for its own use. The more specific the language of the lease relating to alterations and repairs, the less likely are future disputes with the landlord. Depending on the situation, this provision can be as simple as requiring notification of the landlord by the tenant before starting any work, or as complex as a dozen or more pages of construction specifications contained in an exhibit.

If the landlord is providing the initial interior improvements, a simple notification provision is usually adequate for modifications. However, if the landlord is providing a "shell" only, or if the space is located in a shopping mall or a resort, the landlord needs to tightly control the nature and quality of all construction anywhere on the property. This necessitates the use of a detailed list of building standards and specifications, usually contained in an exhibit referred to as "design and construction criteria," "tenant's building requirements," or something similar. In addition, the lease usually imposes an obligation on the tenant to finish construction in a timely manner.

Typically, these exhibits will allow the landlord to approve the architect, contractor, floor plans and construction schedules. Materials lists are scrutinized, and specifications for the mechanical, plumbing, and electrical systems are detailed. Ceilings, floorings, wall coverings, color selections, interior partitioning, and store fronts are made subject to the landlord's review and approval. (If your store front includes a lot of glass, be sure to inform your insurance agent. Replacing glass can be very expensive!) To avoid expensive surprises, tenants are well-advised to review these schedules and specifications with their prospective contractor *before* signing the lease .

While the tenant can do little to modify these provisions, an effort should be made to impose an obligation on the landlord for making timely plan reviews, and to make sure that the landlord's modification requests are not frivolous .

8.03 REQUIRED INVESTMENT OF LESSEE (H)

As an inducement for the landlord to negotiate a lease, a tenant sometimes agrees to make a certain dollar amount of leasehold improvements. Usually the landlord specifies exactly which improvements will be constructed. Most often, they will be components that are to remain after the tenant leaves — mechanical, electrical, plumbing, fire sprinklers, etc. The landlord usually reserves the right to approve plans and cost estimates before construction starts, and to require that all work to be done with proper building permits.

Where the tenant is given a fixed amount of time to complete such improvements before rent commences, the tenant should be clear about the time required for local planning and building permit processes prior to committing to such a provision (see provision 2.04, "Commencement of Rent")

8.04 PROTECTION AGAINST LIENS (M)

Subcontractors, laborers, and material suppliers have the right to protect their claim for payment by filing "mechanic's liens" against the property. This is usually true even if the general contractor has been paid in full, but the general contractor fails to pay the "subs" or suppliers.

It sounds preposterous to have to pay a subcontractor after having paid the general, but it happens. I once went through a three month episode to rectify just such a problem in the middle of building a shopping center. The contractor was using our money to pay off debts on his *previous* job!

To obtain a lien against a property, the contractor, subcontractor, or supplier has to go to court and prove the owner's default in payment for services or materials. Some states have a "recovery fund" from which to reimburse owners up to statutory limits for damages, if the contractor was licensed by that state.

The landlord does not want his property encumbered for construction or repair costs incurred by the tenant. Since mechanic's liens date back to the beginning of the construction job, a landlord working on construction financing wants absolute assurance that no liens will precede a potential mortgage, because a lender simply will not fund a loan behind previously recorded encumbrances.

In some states, it is possible to negotiate a "no lien contract" with the general contractor. When this type of contract is recorded, all subcontractors are bound by its terms, unless the original contract is substantially modified. The lease might require that such contracts be used if possible. Landlords should check out this possibility with their attorneys.

Otherwise, the lease will normally contain a provision requiring the tenant to obtain lien releases in form and content satisfactory to the landlord, and to provide a "performance and payment bond" to guarantee completion and payment of all potential liens. (The premium runs about 5% of the building cost on average.) Otherwise, the tenant will be required to discharge the liens within a given number of days, usually thirty or less. If it becomes necessary for the landlord to discharge mechanics liens, the lease usually converts the amount paid by the landlord to rent due from the tenant, with interest, until the total amount is paid.

Tenants should be very careful about approving construction contracts, especially if they are in a hurry to move in. It may be better to try to renegotiate the lease terms with the landlord if a serious construction problem arises, rather than sign an ill-begotten building contract.

At any rate, the tenant's contractor should be required to record a "notice of completion" with the County Recorder immediately after any work is finished. This will usually prevent any liens from being claimed after forty-five days from publication of the notice. In addition, the tenant might be required to withhold a "retention payment," often amounting to 10% of the contract price, until expiration of the 45-day notice period.

8.05 ALTERATIONS BELONG TO LANDLORD (H)

This clause reaffirms that any improvements constructed within the premises become part of the landlord's building at lease expiration. Consequently, tenants should be careful to differentiate "trade fixtures" from alterations on their construction plans (see provision 3.04, "Surrender").

8.06 RIGHT TO CURE TENANT'S DEFAULT (M)

If after notification by the landlord to do so, the tenant fails to make repairs for which it is responsible, the landlord can make the repairs and charge the tenant for the cost. This provision is especially important in multi-tenant buildings where the landlord is responsible for providing "quiet enjoyment" to other tenants.

8.07 ADDITIONAL PARKING REQUIREMENTS (M)

In most municipalities, the number of parking spaces required is related to the building's square footage. If a tenant constructs a mezzanine within the premises, or otherwise increases the square footage of the building, it is possible that the landlord will be faced with an increased parking requirement. In this case, most leases cause the tenant to participate with the landlord in rectifying the problem, through a direct assessment, or some periodic sharing of the cost for such parking facilities.

8.08 TAX IMPLICATIONS OF ALTERATIONS (M)

Several situations are important with regard to taxes. First, if tenant improvements are extensive and costly, it is likely that the tax assessor will become aware of them when the building permit is issued, and subsequently increase the building's assessed value. Most leases call for a direct increase in the real property tax payment of the tenant responsible for the increase if this occurs. Table 1 illustrates the point.

TABLE 1

EFFECT OF EXTENSIVE IMPROVEMENTS
ON PROPERTY TAXES

- Assume the current assessed valuation is $2,000,000.

- Assume a tenant obtains a building permit for $1,000,000 of new improvements.

- Assume the assessed value is increased by 80% of the cost of the improvements.

	BEFORE	AFTER
Assessed Value		
Tax Rate per Hundred	$ 2,000,000	$ 2,800,000
Tax Amount per Year	$ 3.00	$ 3.00
	$ 60,000	$ 84,000

It would be unfair to assess other tenants in the building for the $24,000 direct tax increase caused by the new improvements.

Tomato and Turnip went to audit. . .

Another problem relates to *income* taxes for the *tenant*. If there is a renewal option, and the remainder of the initial term upon completion of construction is *less than* 60% of the useful life of the improvements, or, if there is a "reasonable certainty" that the option will be exercised, the *option period* will have to be *included* in the "amortization period." This, of course, could significantly reduce the tenant's depreciation deduction, which would increase income taxes (see Table 2 on next page).

Finally, carefully worded language is needed to describe the condition of property "reverting to the landlord." The court's attitude is that depreciation is supposed to protect a taxpayer from loss, not provide a profit. Accordingly, tenants can be required to "maintain" property in "good repair." But a provision requiring the tenant to replace certain assets, or language prohibiting *any* deterioration of the property might invalidate depreciation deductions for the landlord. If the landlord has accumulated $500,000 in depreciation deductions that were later "invalidated," at a 30% tax rate, his tax liability would be $150,000! Oops!!

I know this is a long-winded explanation, and I'm sorry. But that's the way taxes are! The point is, if you are paying for leasehold improvements, *before* making the improvements, consult your accountant or attorney regarding the tax implications. You'll avoid surprises later on.

TABLE 2

POTENTIAL TAX EFFECT
OF A RENEWAL OPTION

Column A: Remaining term is *less than* 60% of useful life or there is reasonable certainty of option exercise.

Column B: Remaining term is 60% *or more* of useful life, or there is *no* reasonable certainty of option exercise.

	Column A	Column B
1) Useful Life of TI's	10	10
Years Remaining on Initial Term After Construction	5	6
Remaining Term as percentage of Useful Life	50	60
2) Yrs. Remaining	5	6
Option Period Years	+ 10	+ 0
Amortization Period	15	6
3) Impvt. Amount	$ 100,000	$ 100,000
Divide by # Yrs.	15	6
Depr. Allowance	$ 6,666	$ 16,666
x Tax Rate	30%	30%
Tax Saving/Yr.	$ 2,000	$ 5,000

GROUP 9

COMMON AREA

LANDLORD'S POSITION:

This is a good place to discuss the "net lease" versus the "gross lease." "Gross" has nothing to do with the landlord's manners. The terms refer to the payment of real estate taxes, casualty insurance, and common area maintenance (CAM). They are all costs of doing business for the landlord. As in other businesses (and, according to the "Gold Rule"), operating costs are passed along to the customer. At issue, though, is the mechanics of *how* they are allocated, and there are several ways, as you'll see.

The "contract rent," or, "fixed minimum" rent, does *not* include charges for these items in a "net" lease, whereas in a "gross" lease they *are* included. Typically, a single-tenant building will operate under a net lease, and a multi-tenant building under a gross lease—but not always. It all depends on how the landlord chooses to operate the building(s) and manage the accounting. Some landlords use a "modified gross" lease in which a budget amount for taxes, insurance, and maintenance is included in the monthly rent. Any difference between the actual costs and the budgeted amount is billed to the tenant periodically (monthly, quarterly, or annually).

If the landlord elects to include none of the costs in base rent, it is considered to be a "triple net" lease. Sometimes taxes will be included, but not insurance or maintenance, which is referred to as a "double net" lease. The terminology can get confusing, so any time you hear the term "net," you would be wise to ask for a definition.

TENANT'S POSITION:

There are two important points for the tenant to consider. One is to define how property taxes, insurance and maintenance costs are to be paid. Taxes are covered in "Group 5," and insurance under "Group 10," so this section will concentrate on maintenance charges.

The common area is most simply defined as all parts of the landlord's property *not* included in the demised (leased) premises. While the exact description varies with each property, it normally includes:

Parking areas, landscaped and recreation areas, sidewalks and pedestrian ways, corridors, lobbies, roofs and roof structures, public seating areas, public washrooms, public drinking fountains, common conference rooms, stairs, public elevators and escalators, loading docks, utility buildings, and exterior building surfaces.

Common area expenses include all costs for repair and maintenance of the common area elements. Some leases include *capital expenditures* when they are required by insurance underwriters for the maintenance or reduction of insurance premiums, or when mandated by changes in laws or local building ordinances. Retrofitting a building with fire sprinklers or energy-saving materials would be examples. Many leases include a surcharge by the landlord (e.g., 10 to 15 percent of the costs) for administration of the common area maintenance.

The second major consideration for the tenant (and the landlord) is the definition of "base year." In some leases, tenants are charged for the difference between the *current year* and *base year* maintenance costs. This can lead to sizable increases in rent.

In a newly-developed building, for instance, the initial leases usually are made before the building is fully-assessed for property tax purposes. During the construction period, the property is often still assessed as *vacant land*, so taxes are far less than after the building is finished. Accordingly, the tenant should insist that the base year be defined as the first "fully-assessed" tax year. Otherwise, the tenant should expect a whopping increase during the second year!

For example, assume an acre of land valued at $5.00 per square foot, is assessed at 80% of market value, and its tax rate is $4.00 per hundred. The taxes will be roughly $6,970.00 per year.

Now assume the owner develops a 15,000 square foot building on the lot, and leases it for $1.00 per square foot per month net. If the net income is capitalized at 10%, and is assessed the next year at 80% of market value at the same tax rate of $4.00 per hundred, the new taxes will be $57,600.00! (see Table 3, next page).

Any way you figure it, that's a whopping increase!!! It behooves both parties to define the "base year" carefully. Occasionally, a landlord will agree to "cap," or limit, the amount of annual tax increases, but not often, since they are a cost over which the landlord has no direct control.

TABLE 3

Comparison Of Property Taxes
Between
Construction-Year Value
And Fully-Assessed Value

1) Construction Year - Vacant Land Assessment:

1 acre — Sq. Ft.		43,560
Fair Market Value per Sq.Ft.		$ 5.00
Fair Market Value	$	217,800
Assessment Rate		80%
Assessed Value	$	174,240
Tax Rate per Hundred		$ 4.00
Annual Taxes	$	6,970

2) First Fully-Assessed Year:

Building Sq. Ft.		15,000
"Net" Rent per Sq. Ft.		$ 1.00
"Net" Rent per Month	$	15,000
Months per Year		12
"Net" Rent per Year	$	180,000
Divide by Cap Rate		10%
Fair Market Value	$	1,800,000
Assessment Rate		80%
Assessed Value	$	1,440,000
Tax Rate per Hundred		$ 4.00
Annual Taxes	$	57,600

COMMONLY INCLUDED PROVISIONS:

9.01 DEFINITION OF FLOOR AREA (H)

This was covered in the discussion of taxes, provision 5.02, "Pro-Rata Share." Normally, the same percentage is used for allocation of all expenses charged to tenants, including common area maintenance.

9.02 INCREASES IN FLOOR AREA (M)

If the landlord constructs additional space in the building or complex, a new common area maintenance budget should be developed and the tenant's pro-rata share of those costs should be adjusted accordingly (see provision 8.07).

If another tenant builds space which causes an increase in common area maintenance costs (or in taxes and insurance), that tenant should be charged a disproportionate share sufficient to cover the increased costs, and the other tenants' pro-rata share adjusted to cover the remaining costs.

9.03 MAINTENANCE CHARGES (H)

If the rent was quoted as a "gross" amount, the language of this clause should provide for allocation of costs related strictly to the common area, and not for repairs to the "structural elements" if they are the landlord's responsibility (see provision 8.01, "Structural Repairs By Landlord"). Be sure the negotiated base rent is properly stated as "gross" or "net" (as discussed under "Landlord's Position" on page 87).

"Base year" also becomes important in this provision. In cases where the landlord is responsible for operating and maintaining the common area, an annual budget is made. Monthly rents are based on budgeted cost estimates, usually for a calendar year. At the end of the year, the landlord computes the actual operating costs for the property and invoices tenants for their proportionate amount of actual costs in excess of the budget, or in rare cases issues a credit for a surplus.

Here's the rub. In a brand new multi-tenant "spec" building (built on speculation without tenants), the first year expenses will be less than usual because the occupancy rate is below 100% during the "lease-up" period. Similarly, if the occupancy rate for an existing building significantly drops, the operating costs will be less than normal for that year. If operating costs for such years are used as "base year" costs, the tenant could easily be overcharged in the following year.

As with real estate taxes (see Table 3), if the tenant is responsible for increases in common area costs above a base year, the base year should be established as the first year of full occupancy. An alternative is to provide that each tenant's pro-rata share is computed as the total common area costs multiplied by the occupancy rate (see Table 4, next page). The tenant should include these charges as "Occupancy Costs" (see Exhibit F).

Landlord's are slightly more inclined to agree to a "cap" on the amount of annual increases in operating expenses —as opposed to taxes and insurance adjustments— because they have more control over the budget for these costs.

Some landlords hire their own maintenance staff. Their lease will provide that labor, workmen's compensation insurance premiums, and depreciation for tools and equipment are included in common area charges. However, depreciation on "structures, facilities, and equipment" should be excluded from common area charges. If building depreciation is included as a common area expense, the tenant is not only "maintaining" the property, he is in effect "replacing" it. As stated in provision 8.08, the landlord should be careful not to invalidate his depreciation deductions because of a poorly worded lease.

TABLE 4

EFFECT OF BASE YEAR SELECTION UNDER A HYPOTHETICAL MONTHLY "CAM" BUDGET

OPERATING COSTS	At 50% Occupancy	At 100% Occupancy
Administration	$ 900	$ 1,000
Gas	600	1,000
Electric	1,800	2,500
Water	400	900
Janitor Service	2,100	3,500
Repairs & Maintenance.	250	350
Operating Costs	$ 6,050	$ 9,250
Insurance	200	200
Taxes	100	500
Total Common Area Costs	$ 6,350	$ 9,950

In this hypothetical example:

1) If "base year" expenses were set at the 50% instead of 100% occupancy levels, "CAMs" would be approximately 57% higher! [($ 9,950 - $ 6,350) / $ 6,350].

2) If 100% occupancy "CAM" costs were allocated on an actual occupancy rate of 50%, "CAM" charges would be 50% less ($ 9,950 × 50% = $ 4,975).

Obviously, establishing the "base year" and the method of allocating pro-rata share of common area expenses means a lot of money to both parties.

9.04 ALLOCATION OF REAL PROPERTY TAXES (H)

This subject was covered in provision 5.02, "Pro-Rata Share" of taxes. Many times, especially under "gross" leases, the provision is included in the "common area" section because it is an expense which is allocated among all tenants in the building or complex.

It is possible for one tenant to construct exotic or extensive improvements causing the property tax assessment to increase dramatically. To protect against that possibility, the lease should provide that if such an event occurs, an adjustment will be made in the computation of the pro-rata shares, passing the increase directly to the tenant causing it (see provision 8.08).

9.05 JANITOR SERVICE (H)

Office buildings and retail centers commonly include janitor service as part of the contract rent, usually referred to as "fully-serviced" rent, but not always. Since the price of cleaning contracts is usually negotiated on a square foot basis, the service is usually included in common area charges.

The extent of cleaning service provided can vary dramatically, and the frequency can be any number of days per week. Tenants should be sure the service included is adequate for their needs, or they are bound to experience another "oh, by the way" type of cost...

9.06 EXTRAORDINARY CHARGES (M)

The lease should provide that if any tenant uses a part of the common area necessitating unusual or extraordinary repairs or maintenance, those costs will be charged directly to the tenant incurring the costs and deducted from the total common area expenses.

9.07 DISPOSAL OF RUBBISH (H)

Garbage and trash collection service is usually included in the common area expenses. However, if the tenant has excessive amounts of refuse, or trash that needs special handling, the landlord will generally require the tenant to make special arrangements for trash collection, and pay for them too!

9.08 PARKING & OTHER JOINT-USE AREAS (M)

Parking is always a problem! Most municipalities have parking ordinances which dictate the number of spaces required for a given number of square feet of rentable space (the parking ratio). For the landlord, parking can be either a simple problem if there is plenty of land to work with, or an incredibly expensive one where land is scarce and expensive.

The points to be negotiated are: 1) the number of spaces available to the tenant, 2) whether or not they are designated for the tenant's exclusive use, 3) the proximity of the spaces to the premises, 4) covered vs. uncovered parking, and 5) parking security in terms of guards, fencing and lighting. For office and retail users, additional issues are the availability and cost of employee and visitor parking, whether "validated" parking is used, and the hours of operation of the lot or garage. Make sure the parking situation fits your situation, and include parking fees in "Occupancy Costs" (Exhibit F).

9.09 SIGNS & IMPROPER SIGNS / DIRECTORY (M)

The landlord maintains control over the signage program for one reason — money! Directly or indirectly, signs can enhance the building's bottom line.

Income from leasing rooftops and building sides to advertisers (or tenants!) produces the *direct* return. Buildings with highway or commercial thoroughfare exposure can generate significant advertising income, providing local sign ordinances permit such signage. In order to create this income, the landlord has to retain the rights to use these areas of the building.

Indirectly, signage can pay dividends in a number of ways. If the sign program helps tenants who pay percentage rent achieve higher sales, the landlord receives more rent. If the signage produces an aesthetically pleasing appearance throughout the property, leasing efforts are facilitated, and ultimately the property may fetch a better price upon disposition.

Landlords must be sure that their sign criteria comply with local sign ordinances. *Tenants* should review signage specifications to determine the cost of the program, and more importantly, whether signage will be adequate for the location of the premises in the building or complex.

The number and placement of signs and directories are negotiable points. Most often, the landlord will provide the directory, and the tenant pays the cost of signs, installation, and removal. The landlord often reserves the right to select the sign installation and removal company.

Removal of improper signs will be required at the tenant's expense ("Sorry Junior!").

9.10 DELIVERIES (M)

Most properties have designated shipping and receiving areas in order to minimize construction cost, to enable the landlord to control the appearance of the property, and to organize traffic flows. In some instances, the hours of operation are regulated. The tenant should be aware of the proximity of the delivery areas to the premises, and of the regulations controlling their use as they relate to the tenant's shipping and receiving requirements.

9.11 LANDLORD'S RIGHT TO MODIFY (M)

This provision bears many names among commercial leases. Sometimes it is referred to as "reservation of landlord"; sometimes it is discussed under "tenant's right to use" common areas; and it is sometimes called "landlord's right to modify."

The language of the provision gives the landlord the right to repair, renovate, alter or demolish any element of the common area, at the landlord's sole discretion. The intent is to give the landlord the ability to keep the property modern, marketable, and competitive.

But, as with the "structural alterations" provision (8.01), tenants should examine the impact of this provision on their particular location within the building or complex, and try to negotiate the right to limit alterations if they materially diminish the utility of the premises for their purpose, or to be moved or otherwise compensated by the landlord.

The landlord's right to change the name of the building or complex is also contained in this clause. For a variety of reasons, a new owner may want to use a new name, or, the current owner may want to rename the project after renovation. This provision allows for the name change.

GROUP 10

INSURANCE

LANDLORD'S POSITION:

"Accidents do happen!" And when they do, the landlord wants to be sure there is adequate insurance coverage. Most often, "adequate" is defined as *at least* the amount of the landlord's original loan. In addition, the policy should require the underwriter to cover the *entire* cost of damages in the event of a partial loss.

The insurance provision usually requires the tenant to insure both the landlord and the property against risks inherent in the operation of the tenant's business. Liability insurance covers the landlord against the injury or damage claims of third parties. Casualty insurance covers "direct" losses to the property, but not the "consequential" loss of rental income, which requires a special indorsement or a separate policy.

In our litigious society, any time something happens on or around someone's property, attorneys look for "deep pockets" to tap. The landlord can count on being named in a suit any time there is an accident on the property. Indemnity provisions protect the landlord from financial loss in these situations.

In a "net" lease, the tenant is usually required to obtain and pay for insurance coverage satisfactory to the landlord. In a "gross" lease, the landlord obtains the coverage and pays the premiums, then bills the tenant(s) for the pro-rata share. If there is a ground lease or a loan on the property, the lease will require the ground lessor and the lender to be named as "additional insureds" at the landlord's cost.

TENANT'S POSITION:

Protection against loss of physical assets, loss of profits because of business interruption, and protection against claims of others who have suffered injury or property damage (liability) are the tenant's primary concerns.

"Leasehold" insurance compensates a tenant for the difference between the rent in a new facility versus the existing one. The cost of insurance premiums compared to the amount of your current rent, trends in market rents, and the proximity and supply of alternative buildings determine the advisability of obtaining the coverage. Consult your insurance agent for availability and premium cost, and a competent real estate broker for local supply and demand conditions.

Since the tenant pays insurance premiums, the cost of insurance coverage is very important. Fortunately, as limits increase the cost per $1,000 tends to decrease. I always recommend that the tenant give a copy of the insurance provisions to its insurance agent, and ask for a cover letter cross-referencing the policy to the lease to be sure that each item is covered.

COMMONLY INCLUDED PROVISIONS:

10.01 INDEMNITY (M)

Also referred to as the "hold harmless" clause, this provision says that the tenant will pay any cost incurred by the landlord as a result of the tenant's use and occupancy of the premises. It includes claims of third persons for death, injury, or property damage caused by acts, omissions, negligence, or breach of any lease provision by the tenant, or anyone associated with the tenant, in or around the leased premises.

Most leases provide that in the event a law suit is filed against the tenant in which the landlord is also named, the tenant must pay for legal counsel satisfactory to the landlord, and to testify or provide affidavits in the landlord's defense. The tenant also assumes responsibility for any economic loss due to fire and other catastrophes within the demised premises, and for losses due to business interruption.

The safest way for the landlord to secure this indemnification is to require the tenant to pay for insurance coverage against these perils.

10.02 POLICY FORM (M)

The landlord wants to be assured not only that adequate insurance coverage is in place, but also that the underwriter will actually be able to pay claims in time of crisis. Consequently, it is common to see a lease require certain financial and performance ratings on insurance companies issuing policies to tenants. Landlords and tenants should check with their attorneys and insurance brokers to clarify this provision in terms of what's legal in their state, and common in their marketplace.

Moreover, the lease commonly requires the tenant to provide the landlord with periodic "certificates of insurance" (e.g. on the anniversary date of lease commencement) naming the landlord, any ground lessor, and any lenders as an "additional insureds" in case a claim is filed.

A "notice of cancellation or lapse" of a tenant's insurance from the underwriter to the landlord, or, a notice of a reduction in the amount of insurance carried by the tenant, is also commonly required.

Most often if the tenant has a "blanket" insurance policy the landlord will accept inclusion under it in lieu of a separate policy. This can sometimes save a tenant heaps of premiums.

10.03   FIRE & CASUALTY   (H)

The most commonly used type of building insurance is "fire and extended coverage." Extended coverage includes such perils as windstorms, hail, explosion, riots and civil commotion, smoke, sprinkler leaks, and damage caused by vehicles and aircraft. If the tenant is providing the policy, the lease will require that the landlord, any lenders, and any ground lessors be named as "additional insureds."

Every area has its own catastrophic hazard. Floods, hurricanes, tornados, and earthquakes can destroy property in an instant. Be sure to review coverage of special hazards with your insurance agent. Never assume a peril is covered.

The landlord should always insist that the building be insured for its *full value,* since the precise *replacement cost* is difficult to fix. Though a tenant may wish to reduce his insurance premiums by reducing the coverage to the "80% co-insurance level" (i.e. where the tenant assumes responsibility for the remaining 20% of the loss), most landlords *and nearly all lenders* will insist on an amount that covers the *full value* of the building. The landlord and lender would simply have too much at risk if the tenant failed to fulfill its responsibility.

As mentioned in the "alterations" group, glass and glazing should be separately insured if the building elevation(s) make extensive use of glass. It is a good idea to discuss coverage of any other special building features with your agent.

10.04 PUBLIC LIABILITY & PROPERTY DAMAGE (H)

Most leases require the tenant to have liability coverage against claims of third parties that arise from the tenant's use and occupancy of the premises. In addition, a prudent landlord will establish the right to periodically set coverage limits commensurate with risk levels, and insist that the tenant bear the cost for including the landlord, ground lessor, and lenders as additional insureds.

Beware of third party claims!

10.05 CONTENTS OF DEMISED PREMISES (H)

Improvements permanently affixed to the building become the property of the landlord. The tenant's ability to pay rent depends on the use of improvements, plus trade fixtures, equipment, and merchandise, i.e., "contents." (Trade fixtures are items of personal property affixed to the building, needed to conduct business, but removable by the tenant).

Consequently, the lease usually requires the tenant to maintain insurance on leasehold improvements and "contents," for the full amount of their undepreciated replacement cost, against the same perils covered under the fire and extended coverage policy, and any special perils. In addition, coverage against vandalism and malicious mischief is usually required. This provision is some-times labeled "assumption of risk," or something similar. (See also provision 17.23, "Insurance — Fixtures & Merchandise.")

The lease stipulates that proceeds from any insurance claim are to be used to expeditiously replace damaged improvements, and that if proceeds are inadequate to cover replacement, the tenant pays the additional cost. Further, if the premises are damaged beyond repair, the lease generally states that the landlord will receive insurance proceeds equal to the value of the leasehold improvements. Tenants, be sure to show this clause to your insurance agent!

10.06 CERTIFICATION OF COSTS (M)

Sometimes included in "alterations and repairs," and sometimes not included at all, this provision calls for the tenant to provide the landlord, on an annual basis, a written certification of the replacement cost of *leasehold improvements* not included in a previous certification. In other words, how much money did you spend on improvements this year? This certification is used to determine insurance limits for the fire and extended coverage policy.

10.07 LIABILITY FOR INCREASED PREMIUMS (M)

Fire insurance premiums take into consideration the degree of hazard attendant to various uses within the building. The use of hazardous construction materials, and storage of combustible or toxic materials can cause dramatic increases in fire insurance premiums. Whether or not the landlord consents to such use, a tenant precipitating a premium increase should expect to pay for it.

10.08 OVERLOADING ELECTRICAL SYSTEM (M)

Occasionally, insurance underwriters send inspectors to examine an insured building. Occasionally, they find a tenant who has installed equipment that stresses the electrical system far in excess of the original design, thus creating a fire hazard. This provision imposes the duty on the tenant to rectify the problem, or to pay the increased premiums.

10.09 KEY MAN (H)

In situations where the success of the business is critically dependent on one or more of its principals (e.g. an artist), the landlord might require the tenant to purchase this life insurance with proceeds designated for payments due under the lease. It's similar to a security deposit.

10.10 BOILER (H)

The use of a boiler for heating generally triggers the need for special insurance, and special insurance premiums. If your building will use one, check out the premium with your agent .

10.11 WAIVER OF SUBROGATION (M)

This an awful sounding thing. I don't know why they couldn't have found a more pleasant name. But it's really a simple provision to understand.

Suppose the landlord provides the fire insurance policy, but the tenant insures its contents and leasehold improvements through a different company. Insurance companies hate to pay claims. If a claim arises the company that has to settle the claim would like the ability to collect the settlement from the other party.

This means that if the landlord's carrier paid the claim it could collect from the tenant, and vice versa! What a deal! Charge your customer a premium, pay a claim, then recoup the loss from the other party. Pure profit for the insurance company, and a nightmare for the insured parties.

"Subrogation" means substituting one party for the other. Waiver of subrogation means that the insured agrees not to allow its insurance carrier to seek redress from the other party if a claim is paid. In other words, the insurance policy will *not* contain a subrogation clause. To be fair, this waiver should be mutual between the landlord and the tenant. See, I told you it was simple!

GROUP 11

Assignment & Subletting

LANDLORD'S POSITION:

For the landlord, both sub-letting and assignment are merely nuisances caused by changes in the tenant's circumstances. The fundamental issue is control of the property. Ownership gives the landlord the right to control what uses occur on the property, as well as what financial, credit, and ethical standards to apply to tenants. Without restrictions on transfer of leasehold interests, the landlord would literally be stuck with *whomever the tenant chose to substitute*. And as we go on, you will see that the right to restrict transfer can become very profitable for the landlord.

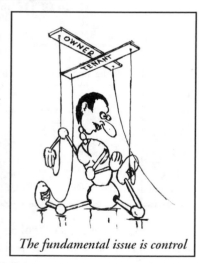

The fundamental issue is control

There are usually no tax consequences of assignment or subletting to the landlord, as long as the rental obligation remains unchanged under the prime lease.

TENANT'S POSITION:

Things don't always go as planned. Economic downturns can ruin a business. Markets change, and companies change their business strategies. New properties are developed, changing the relative attractiveness of a particular location. A buyer makes a tenant an offer too good to be refused. For these reasons and many more, tenants want *and need* the flexibility to terminate their obligations before the lease actually expires. *How* the tenant chooses to do this will affect two things: 1) the degree of ongoing obligation, and 2) the tax consequences.

Effects of Transfer Choices

	Sublease	Assignment	Cancellation
Original Tenant	Primary Obligation	No Obligation	No Obligation
New Tenant	Secondary Obligation	Primary Obligation	N/A
Original Lease	Unchanged	Unchanged	Cancelled
New Contract	Sublease	Assignment of Lease	Cancellation Agreement

The tenant's tax consequences of an assignment versus a sublease should always be examined *before* the existing lease is transferred or the sublease is signed. An assignment will normally be treated as a sale of a capital asset, and payments received are treated as capital gains. Similarly, any penalties are simply treated as capital losses. In a sublease, if the rent is *higher* than the prime lease rent, the difference will be *ordinary income* to the tenant. If the sublease rent is *lower* than the prime rent, the tenant will have an *operating loss*. In this case, depending on his individual tax circumstances, the tenant may want to negotiate a cancellation

TABLE 5

Comparison Of Tax Consequences
Sublease versus Cancellation

SUBLEASE (OPERATING LOSS) SCENARIO:

ASSUMPTIONS:

1) Prime lease is $5,000 per month with 5 years remaining
2) Sublease is $4,000 per month for the balance of the term

[1]Annual Prime Lease Rent	$ 60,000
[2]Annual Sublease Rent	-48,000
Annual Operating Loss*	$ 12,000

CANCELLATION SCENARIO:

ASSUMPTIONS:

1) The existing tenant desires a *large* tax deduction in the current year, and would like to eliminate the contingent liability under the existing lease
2) New tenant will pay initial rent of $4,000 per month on a new 10 year lease
3) The Landlord hires a broker to find a subtenant (but the original tenant pays).
4) The Landlord hires an attorney to draft the documents (tenant pays again).

Existing Prime Lease Rent	$ 60,000
[2]New Lease Rent	− 48,000
Annual Rent Decrease	12,000
Years Remaining on Existing Lease	× 5
Total Rent Loss	$60,000
[3]Brokerage Commission	+ 10,000
[4]Legal and Closing Costs	+ 5,000
[1]Tenant's Cancellation Penalty*	$ 75,000

- Under the cancellation scenario, the original tenant's tax savings in the current year would be more than six times larger than under the sublease scenario.

- Also under the cancellation scenario, the Landlord ends up with a new tenant for ten years without rent loss or leasing expenses.

NOTE: The "time value" of money (compound interest), or present value, was ignored intentionally for the sake of simplicity.

*The original tenant's applicable tax rate determines the tax savings.

with the landlord, thereby converting the operating loss for the remainder of the lease term into a *one-time loss* deductible *in one tax year* instead. Table 5 on the previous page shows why (also see provision 11.06).

COMMONLY INCLUDED PROVISIONS:

11.01 LANDLORD'S CONSENT REQUIRED (M)

In an "assignment," all rights and obligations in the lease are transferred to another party (the assignee), and the primary (transferring) tenant (the assignor) has no ongoing responsibility. Under a "sublease," the primary tenant (the sublessor) remains responsible to the landlord, and the subtenant is responsible to the primary tenant.

An important consideration in the decision of most landlords to sign a lease is the financial ability of the tenant to pay rent and maintain the property. Therefore, any "change of control" of tenancy is closely scrutinized. The landlord wants to know "who he's doing business with." Transfer of the majority interest in corporations or partnerships, mergers, acquisitions, consolidations, and court-ordered reorganizations of the tenant require the landlord's consent for transfer of the leasehold interest.

Every transfer must be approved separately. A violation of this provision usually gives the landlord the option to accept the new occupant, or, to terminate the lease after giving notice to the tenant. Legal and administrative costs incurred by the landlord in connection with a lease transfer will be charged to the original tenant.

11.02 LANDLORD'S OPTIONS (M)

When the issue of assignment or sublease arises, it is most often initiated by the tenant for the tenant's benefit. This puts landlords on the defensive to protect their interests. They are anxious to get rid of bad tenants, but hate to lose good ones. The landlord cannot "unreasonably" withhold consent to a transfer, or a lawsuit is likely. As a result, the lease should spell out the need for written notification to the landlord by the tenant, the need for the tenant to be in full compliance with all covenants of the lease to qualify for the privilege to transfer, and set guidelines to be used in evaluating the suitability of a subtenant or assignee.

It is reasonable for the landlord to insist that a substitute tenant have financial capability at least equal to the tenant's, and therefore to require a recent set of financial statements, a credit report, and perhaps a binder or certificate of liability insurance. Guidelines should relate liquid assets and/or profit levels of the proposed tenant to the total rent and other financial obligations under the lease. The more detailed the language of this provision, the less likely are disputes.

11.03 LANDLORD'S RIGHT TO PURCHASE (M)

A variety of circumstances can add significant value to the leasehold. The tenant would like to cash in on these situations, but most leases make it difficult to do so.

Changes in the location value of the property, inflation, or supply and demand conditions can cause *market* rents to climb much higher than the tenant's current *contract* rent, creating a potential profit for the tenant. To prevent tenants from "getting into the real estate business," most leases contain a provision entitling the landlord to recapture *all (but not part)* of the tenant's space at the *lower* of the applicable rent due under the lease, or the rent which the tenant proposes to get.

If there is a lot of time remaining on the initial term, or if the tenant has attractive renewal (or purchase) options, the lease may also be *salable* to another party. If *market* rents are *higher* than the *contract* rent, the landlord *will* most likely exercise the option to recapture and relet the space at the higher rent. If *market* rent is *below* (or equal to) *contract* rent, the landlord will most likely *not* exercise the option.

Also, a tenant who has made extensive improvements to the property and has an attractive lease may want to sell its lease or business. The parties will then want to include leasehold improvements in the transaction. But remember, the improvements already belong to the landlord under the "Alterations & Repairs" provision!

Here comes the "Gold Rule" again! This time it's called "Apportionment of Sale Proceeds," or "Lessor's Right to Purchase," or something similar. The provision states, in essence, that if the tenant decides to sell its leasehold interest, or to sell its business, the landlord has an option to buy it first.

There are as many formulas for establishing the landlord's option price as there are landlords. In an outright purchase, a commonly used method is for the landlord to

*"It's mine." "No, it's **mine!**"*

match the terms and conditions of a bona fide offer, less the amount the landlord would normally charge for consent to an assignment. The consent to an assignment or sublease will usually be based on something similar to one of the following:

1) Tenant pays the landlord the depreciated value of leasehold improvements.

2) Tenant pays any unpaid amounts for leasehold improvements made by the landlord on behalf of the tenant.

3) Tenant pays the greater of a fraction of the purchase price (half; three fourths), less brokerage commissions and closing costs, or, the undepreciated value of leasehold improvements.

(see Table 6 on next page)

11.04 CANCELLATION NOT MERGER (M)

This provision usually gives *the landlord* the option to decide what happens in the event of a cancellation of the primary lease. Sometimes a tenant has created one or more subleases and subsequently decides to "surrender" (terminate) its lease, or the landlord elects to cancel the lease for violation of a lease provision (like not paying rent!). He may choose to terminate any or all of those subleases, or to *assign* those leases to himself, thereby eliminating the sub-lessee. Therefore, a sub-lessee should make sure that the sub-lessor handles all lease obligations responsibly, or he could find himself "taking a fall" as the carpet is pulled out from under him!

11.05 NO OBLIGATION TO RENEW (M)

Usually found under "Assignment & Subletting," but sometimes as a separate provision such as "Renewal," this seemingly innocent clause can be a killer to the tenant. It simply states that the landlord may refuse to give the tenant a new lease when it expires. No problem if it's a small space, or a short term, and the tenant had no long-term intentions about the space.

TABLE 6

ESTABLISHING THE LANDLORD'S PURCHASE PRICE

1) IF TENANT PAYS FOR IMPROVEMENTS:

Initial Improvement Cost	$ 100,000
Years in Original Term	÷ 10
Annual Depr. (Straight Line)	10,000
Yrs. Remaining At Time of Sublease	× 3
Consent Fee Paid to Landlord	$ 30,000

The theory is that the improvements belong to the Landlord when the Tenant surrenders the premises.

2) IF LANDLORD PAYS FOR IMPROVEMENTS:

Initial Improvement Cost	$ 100,000
Years in Original Term	10
Annual Interest on Tenant Improvements (TI) Cost	10%
Years Remaining at Time of Sublease	3
Balance Remaining After 7 Years	
(Per Loan Progress Chart from Lender)	
Equals "Consent Fee" paid to Landlord	$ 41,000

3) PURCHASE PRICE vs. UNDEPRECIATED TI's:

Assume Undepreciated TI Value as #1 above	$ 30,000
Assume: Sales Price of	$ 100,000
Negotiated Fraction	× 50%
Fractional Value	$ 50,000
Brokerage Commission	- 10,000
Closing Costs	- 3,000
Net Amount	$ 37,000
Consent Fee Paid To Landlord	$ 37,000

The Tenant *must* understand the impact of this provision on any contemplated transaction so that the terms of the transfer agreement (assignment or sublease) are structured properly.

But if it is a large space in which the tenant has made a heavy investment, or the location has become strategically critical (e.g., a retail site or warehouse facility) the inability to renew can be financially devastating. If the tenant happens to be selling its business near the time the lease expires this provision can be a real problem too.

In one negotiation I remember, a tenant who was trying to sell his business had a lucrative offer from a qualified buyer, conditioned on the tenant's obtaining a lease renewal from the landlord. The lease contained a "non-renewal" clause. It wound up costing the tenant $250,000 cash to induce the landlord to renew the lease! The landlord figured out how much profit the tenant was going to make by selling his business, and took just about all of it. It is not uncommon for this "key money," "incentive," or "premium" rent to reach seven figures.

Sometimes, the landlord just doesn't like the tenant, or another tenant makes him an offer he can't refuse, so the previous tenant loses the space. Longevity is no birthright. Never forget the "Gold Rule!!!"

11.06 NEGOTIATING A CANCELLATION (M)

Rather than suffer through the entire term, the parties to a disadvantageous lease agreement might agree to an early cancellation. The same reasons that lead to an assignment or subletting can trigger an outright cancellation. The difference is that the landlord ends up with the property.

The party originating the cancellation can expect to pay for the privilege. If the landlord wants to cancel, the tenant receives a cancellation "bonus." If the tenant raises the issue, a cancellation "penalty" will be charged. The amount of the settlement is subject to (arduous) negotiation, and depends

TABLE 7

LANDLORD'S TAX CONSEQUENCES FROM CANCELLATION VS. SUBLEASE

<u>LEASE CANCELLATION:</u>

Cancellation Penalty Amount	$ 75,000
Assume:	
Original Brokerage Commission	$ 15,000
Original Bonus Paid to Tenant	10,000
Original Legal & Closing Costs	+ 4,000
Total Lease Acquisition Costs	29,000
Time Remaining on Lease	50%
Unamortized Acquisition Costs	$ 14,500
Taxable Income*	$ 60,500

<u>CONVERT LEASE TO SUBLEASE:</u>

Landlord Wants Penalty Paid Over 5 Years	
Assume:	
Cancellation Penalty Amount	$ 75,000
Months Amortized	÷ 60
Monthly Amortization	$ 1,250
Sublease Rent	+ 5,000
Prime Lease Rent per Month	$ 6,250
Monthly Rent Increase	$ 1,250
	× 12mo.
Increase in Annual Taxable Income*	$ 15,000

• Final tax amount will depend on the landlord's tax rate.

on the motivation of each party to cancel, their financial capability, and how much they really know about each other's situation.

No matter who pays whom, both parties should seek tax counsel early on. As always, the tax consequences of the transaction can be very complicated. Competent counsel can often facilitate negotiations, and usually produce a tax result beneficial to both parties. Tax laws change continually, but the following are some general guidelines currently in effect.

LANDLORD'S CANCELLATION CONSIDERATIONS:

Cancellation penalties and forfeited security deposits paid to the landlord by the tenant are considered as additional rent to the landlord and taxed as ordinary income, after deducting any unamortized costs of making the lease, such as brokerage commissions, attorney's fees, incentive bonuses, and closing costs.

To mitigate this tax bite, the landlord could arrange for the canceling tenant to sublease to a new tenant and spread the penalty over a number of years by raising the prime and/or the sublease rent. Of course, the tenant trying to cancel would not actually terminate its lease in this case, but would become a "sublessor," and would therefore remain "contingently liable" under the lease. His rent problem, however, would disappear (see Table 7 on previous page).

The landlord should never take a penalty from the canceling tenant and then pay it to a new tenant as a bonus, since such an amount is taxable in the year received, but the amount paid out is amortized over the term of the old lease. This could create a decided tax *disadvantage.*

A cancellation bonus paid to a tenant must be amortized by the landlord under the following general guidelines:

- for a new lease to a new tenant, the bonus amortization period normally is the term of the new lease.

- If the landlord is demolishing a building to build a new one, the amortization period of the bonus is usually the life of the new building.

- Where a new tenant will build a new building, the landlord should check with tax counsel. The landlord would prefer the shorter of either the useful life of the building or the lease term. The IRS might feel differently.

- If the landlord takes over the building, the bonus must be amortized over the unused term of the old lease.

TENANT'S CANCELLATION CONSIDERATIONS:

A "bonus" received by a tenant is treated as income when received. If the lease is a capital asset, meaning it was purchased, the bonus is considered as a capital gain. However, where the bonus exceeds the tenant's unamortized cost of acquiring the lease (basis), IRS code section 1250 might convert a portion of the capital gain to ordinary income.

When the landlord owns the building, if a cancellation *penalty* is paid by the tenant it will normally be deductible by the tenant in the year of cancellation.

A special tax consideration arises if the tenant constructed the building on leased property and later buys the land, thereby merging the leasehold and fee interests, which cancels the lease. In this instance the annual tax deduction may change, because instead of deducting the entire lease payments, only depreciation over the remaining useful life of the building can be deducted. The portion of the price allocated to land must be added to the tenant's basis, and recovered upon ultimate disposition. However, mortgage interest can be added to the total deduction which may significantly close the gap.

As Table 8 (next page) shows, the disparity in the tax deduction between owning and leasing will be influenced by:

1) The proportion of the purchase price allocated to the building versus the land;

2) The downpayment and loan amount;

3) The interest rate on the loan;

4) The remaining useful life at the time of purchase;

5) The amount of rent being paid under the lease.

11.07   NOTICE OF INTENT TO MORTGAGE   (M)

A "leasehold mortgage" secures a loan on the leasehold interest of a tenant. It encumbers the *contractual* interest in the premises as well as the *physical* improvements. It therefore becomes an encumbrance on the property, and that always arouses the landlord's interest.

Consequently, most leases contain a provision limiting leasehold mortgages to loans for making or renovating physical improvements *to the premises*. It will commonly require the tenant to use a "recognized lending institution," a term that should be clearly defined in the lease.

It will always require the landlord's written approval of the mortgage instrument. This will enable the landlord to review construction plans (since improvements revert to the landlord), and the tenant's ability to satisfy the terms of the mortgage so as not to jeopardize rent payments.

I included this provision under "Assignment & Subletting" because foreclosure of the leasehold mortgage would trigger a *transfer of interest* in the leasehold estate to the lender.

TABLE 8

COMPARISON OF OWNERSHIP AND LEASE TAX DEDUCTIONS

ASSUME:

1) Building is currently leased at $150,000 per year.

2) Building is purchased after 10 years for $1,500,000 with $375,000 allocated to land, and $1,125,000 to the building.

3) A 70% loan at 9% annual interest.

4) INTEREST DEDUCTION:

Purchase Price	$ 1,500,000
Loan Ratio	× 70%
Loan Amount	$ 1,050,000
Interest Rate	× 9%
Annual Interest	$ 94,500

5) DEPRECIATION DEDUCTION:

Building Allocation	$ 1,125,000
Remaining Useful Life	÷ 30yrs.
Annual Depreciation	$ 37,460

6)

Annual Interest	$ 94,500
Annual Depreciation	+ 37,460
Annual Tax Deduction	$ 131,960
Annual Lease Payment	$ +(150,000)
Decrease in Tax Deduction	$ (18,040)

As you can see, cancellation is simple to conceptualize, but a bit more complicated to effect successfully from a tax standpoint. Consult with your tax attorney or accountant before signing the agreement.

GROUP 12

Default

LANDLORD'S POSITION:

By signing a lease, the landlord becomes dependent on the tenant for an income stream needed to pay operating costs, mortgage payments, and possibly ground rent, all of which carry their own penalties for default. Obviously, the impact of default by the tenant can be devastating to the landlord. Additionally, in a multi-tenant building, the landlord is charged with the responsibility to provide "quiet enjoyment" to all the tenants in the building. The default provision affords the landlord the means to protect his interests should a tenant fail to perform as agreed, whether financially or behaviorally.

CASH FLOW

TENANT'S POSITION:

Despite the optimism and enthusiasm existing at the time a lease is signed, circumstances can change a tenant's ability or willingness to abide by the terms of the agreement. The key point for the tenant is to be aware of the remedies at the landlord's disposal, and to understand their consequences if they are used. Needless to say, the advice of legal counsel regarding the specific language of this provision should be sought before signing the lease.

COMMONLY INCLUDED PROVISIONS:

12.01 DEFAULT BY LANDLORD (M)

Since the landlord drafts the lease, it not surprising to find this to be a rather brief (if not absent) provision. When it *is* included, it usually imposes a duty on the landlord to "diligently" correct a default that is specifically stated in a written notice from the tenant.

12.02 DEFINITION OF TENANT'S DEFAULT (M)

Generally speaking, defaults fall into two categories; financial and behavioral. "Financial default" occurs if the tenant fails to pay minimum or percentage rent, or any amounts included under "additional" rent, or fails to pay on time.

In addition, most leases provide that if the tenant voluntarily or involuntarily becomes involved in a bankruptcy proceeding, or any other reorganization, attachment, or legal proceedings by creditors, and cannot dismiss the proceedings within a given number of days (say, 15 or 30), a default has occurred. Absent such a provision, the landlord might be caught up in legal proceedings for months. Bankruptcy courts "abhor forfeitures," which means that the court is predisposed to protect the debtor (tenant) at great length. So to be effective, the lease must state emphatically that the landlord has the right to terminate the lease immediately. And, if the landlord accepts rent after giving a "notice of cancellation," it could be considered a "waiver" of the default provision.

Any lien or other encumbrance placed on the property without the landlord's consent is defined as a default. Similarly, if a "guarantor" of a lease fails to comply with the terms of the guaranty when called upon to do so by the landlord, this "non-compliance of a guarantor" is also a default. In short, the tenant has the obligation to satisfy its financial obligations so as not to jeopardize the landlord's financial or legal position.

"Behavioral defaults" deal with the tenant's failure to adhere to all other covenants, conditions, and regulations contained in the lease. After written notice from the landlord specifying the cause of default, the tenant is given a certain number of days, usually 15 or 30, within which to cure the default, or at least to begin diligently working on it. Finally, if the tenant vacates the premises without notifying the landlord properly, or removes substantially all its personal property, default has normally occurred also.

12.03 LANDLORD'S REMEDIES (M)

Under the law, landlords generally have a duty to minimize their losses arising from a tenant's default. They cannot just sit back and let damages pile up until they feel like doing something about it. Because of their financial obligations to lenders and other creditors, most landlords are anxious to correct problems that jeopardize their income. The lease details exactly what remedies are available, and how the landlord can proceed in case of a default.

One remedy is to institute eviction proceedings to physically remove the tenant, and if necessary, store abandoned property elsewhere at the tenant's expense. The landlord can reserve the option to either terminate the lease and cancel all rights of the tenant , or to take possession of the premises "for the account of the tenant," without terminating the lease. In the latter instance, the landlord may be permitted to sublease or subdivide the space, and/or to operate the tenant's business until a final judgment from the court is obtained.

In any event, the lease will normally allow the landlord to recover (as damages) reasonable attorney's fees and all costs of re-letting the premises, including alterations, repairs, and brokerage commissions. In addition, if the landlord finds a new tenant and the new rent falls short of the amounts called for in the old lease, the old tenant might be liable for the difference.

12.04 LATE CHARGES (M)

Often included in the Rent clause, this provision actually applies to the tenant's failure to pay rent on a timely basis. Since it is a "penalty" clause, I prefer to include it as a "default" provision. The amount can be a fixed sum, or a percentage of the rent due, and is usually related to the amount of the landlord's penalty for late payment under a financing agreement or ground lease. At any rate, the amount of the late charge will always be high enough to encourage the tenant to pay on time!

12.05 INTEREST ON PAST DUE AMOUNTS (M)

In addition to imposing a late charge, some leases stipulate that any amounts due shall bear interest from the date due until paid in full at the maximum rate allowed by law, or, at a formulated rate based on another published rate (e.g. "Prime + 2%). Here again, the intent is to discourage tenants from "sand bagging," and to reimburse the landlord for his "opportunity cost" of not being able to use the money had it been paid when due.

12.06 LIQUIDATED DAMAGES / CANCELLATION   (M)

In the event the tenant breaches the lease prior to taking possession, or unduly delays taking possession, the lease usually provides that the landlord can upon written notice to the tenant, cancel the agreement and keep the security deposit as liquidated damages.

12.07 NO ACCORD AND SATISFACTION   (M)

This provision states that the tenant cannot unilaterally modify the lease by sending the landlord a rent amount less than the full amount due. If the tenant is late with a payment, a partial payment does not, without the landlord's prior consent *each time,* satisfy its obligations. Even if the tenant accompanies the partial payment with a letter suggesting a new agreement (accord) regarding the rent payment, it does not constitute "satisfaction" of the obligation. If the landlord has served the tenant notice to terminate the lease, or started a suit for summary possession (eviction), the same principles apply.

12.08 WAIVER OF RIGHTS OF REDEMPTION   (M)

Some states have laws that allow a tenant to cure a default during the eviction process. Eviction is always a time-consuming, costly, and unpleasant experience. Once the landlord has begun the process, the landlord/tenant relationship is usually beyond repair. For this reason, some leases contain a waiver of the tenant's right under present or future laws to redeem itself once eviction proceedings are commenced by the landlord.

While the reasoning is understandable from the landlord's point of view, any time a tenant's legal rights are being waived it is wise to seek legal counsel before signing.

12.09 NON-WAIVER / CUMULATIVE REMEDIES   (M)

Just because you get away with something once doesn't mean you can do it all the time. Under this provision, a landlord's decision to accept late rent once, with or without imposing a late charge, does not mean a late rent payment will be acceptable the next time. Similarly, violations of other provisions of the lease that for a time go unnoticed do not stop the landlord from asserting his rights later on (non-waiver). Even so, I'm sure an attorney would advise a prudent landlord to document his objections in writing!

In addition, all the rights and remedies given the landlord by the lease are available at the same time (cumulative). Use of one remedy does not preclude the landlord from using others.

It should be clear by now that the default provisions can invoke a variety of legal proceedings. While a landlord might be skeptical about a tenant who dwells on the default clauses during negotiations, it behooves tenants to understand the legal ramifications of those clauses before signing the lease.

GROUP 13

Destruction Of Building

LANDLORD'S POSITION:

It is difficult to put a square peg in a round hole. A building damaged by fire or other catastrophe may be able to accommodate *some* tenants, but not others. The age, overall condition, specific location and extent of damage determine the advisability of repairing or demolishing the building. Somebody has to make the call. Since the landlord owns the building, he reserves the right to make it.

TENANT'S POSITION:

The best thing a tenant can do is insure itself against losses wrought by destruction of the premises, as discussed in GROUP 10—INSURANCE, and to fully understand the rights and duties of both parties when catastrophe strikes.

COMMONLY INCLUDED PROVISIONS:

13.01 REPAIRS BY TENANT (M)

When damage occurs, the landlord wants the building restored as quickly as possible in order to preserve the earning power of the property and to minimize discomfort to other tenants in the building or complex. The landlord might also have a sale or refinancing contingent on completion of such repairs.

Consequently, the lease most often contains an obligation for the tenant to begin repairs upon notice from the landlord that the building is ready for work, and to complete the work within a prescribed time limit. All improvements, store fronts, equipment, and trade fixtures installed prior to the casualty are required to be restored (see provision 10.06). The tenant will be responsible for all repairs not called for under the landlord's repairs provision (see provision 8.01), reemphasizing the need for a clear definition *in that clause* of each party's responsibility.

13.02 ABATEMENT OF MINIMUM RENT (M)

Most leases will provide for the minimum rent to be reduced from the date damage occurs until the date of its repair. The amount is usually based on the proportionate reduction in useable square footage.

However, the potential loss of business may be much greater than the size of the reduction in square footage. The tenant should examine the building floor plan and site plan to establish his vulnerability to disruption, and, negotiate equitable terms for rent abatement. In addition, if the lease contains a *percentage* rent clause, it too should be reviewed. The landlord will want the gross sales starting limit lowered to coincide with the reduction in minimum rent. Finally, the lease should specify when full rent is to resume, and should give the tenant a reasonable period of time to refixture after the landlord has completed restoration of the building.

13.03 CONTINUATION OF BUSINESS (M)

To the extent reasonable from a "safety and good business" standpoint, the tenant will be required to continue operation of its business. If the tenant can envision any special circumstances under which continuation would be disadvantageous they should be stated in the lease. Construction noise for a recording studio, or loss of power for a surgeon's office are examples of special circumstances.

13.04 TERMINATION OF LEASE (M)

A variety of circumstances can make continuation of the lease after a catastrophe impractical or impossible. Most often, the landlord reserves the sole right to make the decision to terminate the lease. The reasons for cancellation usually spelled out in this provision are:

- The damage or destruction was caused by a risk not insured under the landlord's insurance policies. There will be no money to rebuild. (Oops !!!)

- The landlord's mortgage requires that insurance proceeds are to be applied to reduce the principal balance of the loan. There *could* be nothing left for reconstruction.

- The time remaining on the lease term is too short, or the building is too damaged. The time and damage limits should be negotiated and then specified in the lease. These are usually from 2 to 5 years for the remaining lease term, and damage in excess of 20 percent of the replacement cost.

- The building or common area is damaged beyond a stated percentage, regardless of whether the *tenant's* premises are damaged or not. It is possible for all but a very small portion of a building to be destroyed, in which case it could be more practical to demolish the remainder of the building and start over.

- The tenant's premises *and either the building or the common area* is damaged beyond a specified percentage of replacement cost, usually 25% or more (same reasons as in the preceding paragraph).

- Repairs or reconstruction cannot be completed within a reasonable time (say, 6 months) because of applicable laws or regulations, or other reasons over which the landlord has no control. For instance, if zoning laws were changed after the lease was signed it may be economically impractical or impossible to replace the building or get a permit to rebuild.

The lease will normally require advance written notice of the landlord's decision to terminate, after which the tenant is required to vacate the premises and surrender the lease. It should also provide for a refund of any amounts paid by the tenant but unearned as of the date of the damage that caused the termination.

Obviously, the landlord needs the terms of this provision to be uniform among all tenants of the property. However, the tenant should examine the impact of the provision relative to the size of its contemplated investment (see provision 11.06).

GROUP 14

CONDEMNATION

LANDLORD'S POSITION:

It is important that the language of this provision be tailored to the laws of the state in which the property is located. Some states allow only one condemnation award. Some allow both the landlord *and* the tenant to seek an award.

If the lease is "silent" on the issue of condemnation, the landlord usually will receive only the value of the "fee" minus the value of the "leasehold." The leasehold value would then be paid to the tenant. The "leasehold value" is generally defined as the present value of the "fair market rent," less the present value of the "contract rent" to be paid over the remaining term. Consequently, the commercial lease is rarely "silent" with regards to condemnation, and usually seeks to preserve the entire award for the landlord.

TENANT'S POSITION:

Where the tenant plans to make a substantial investment in the facility over a long-term this provision can be important. Without the ability to share in a condemnation award, the tenant is reluctant to spend a lot of money improving the property. However, for short-term deals with "cookie-cutter" improvements, it has far less relevance.

I have seen numerous negotiations drag on and on over this provision. Most of the time they were silly. Why spend hours of attorney time arguing about condemnation awards on a newly-constructed building in the middle of a pre-planned office or industrial park for a three-year lease?! The point is, with a bit of investigation at the municipality's planning, building, and public works departments, the likelihood of a property ever being condemned can be reasonably ascertained. The intensity of negotiation on this provision should relate to the likelihood of its ever being used.

COMMONLY INCLUDED PROVISIONS:

14.01 TOTAL (PERMANENT) TAKING (M)

If the *entire* property is taken under eminent domain proceedings the obvious consequence is termination of the lease. The primary issues are which party receives the condemnation award, and, how it will be divided between landlord and tenant. As stated earlier, most leases will state simply that if there is only one award it belongs to the landlord.

Where the tenant plans to make costly improvements, a compromise position is to establish a formula for reimbursement of the tenant's unamortized costs. For example, on a 20-year lease, the cost of the tenant improvements could be reduced 5 percent per year.

Some landlords argue that the risk of condemnation is most onerous to the tenant in the early years of the lease when the investment has not been recovered through depreciation deductions or operating profits. In this case, the formula could require the tenant to use an accelerated method of depreciation for the improvements, thus ensuring that the landlord will receive a larger share of an award later in the lease term. Still other landlords assert that under the terms of the "alteration and repairs" provision the improvements belong to them anyhow, so the tenant is entitled to only a "token" amount of the award. (Remember the "Gold Rule"!)

Another issue in total condemnation is the actual date of the lease termination. Eminent domain cases usually take a long time to grind their way through the court -- often years. So, when should the lease end? The solution is "subject to negotiation." The tenant often wants out as early as possible to allow more time for relocation. The landlord, not surprisingly, prefers to collect rent up to the date of the award. In cases where the tenant is to receive a portion of the award, a compromise position is to offset rent foregone by the landlord against the tenant's share of the proceeds (if termination is allowed before the date of the award).

Under any circumstances, the tenant will usually be entitled to seek a *separate* award covering the value of trade fixtures and moving expenses.

14.02 PARTIAL TAKING (M)

Here again, if the lease is silent on this point, the tenant is entitled to reimbursement for the diminished value of the leasehold. The lease, therefore, should address at least the following issues:

• **Allocation of award proceeds:** The same points covered under total taking apply here, except that the *proportion* of proceeds given to each party must be settled.

• **Adjustment of rent:** The fairest solution restores both parties to their original position. Reducing rent based on square footage reductions may not be the most equitable method, since a unit's value can be affected by factors other than square footage.

Perhaps the most equitable way is to reduce the rent by the same percentage that the *market value* of each unit is reduced by the partial taking. In the example below, the building square feet drops 33% while Unit 1's square feet drops 50%. If the landlord adjusted both tenants' rent based on the 33% square foot reduction, Unit 1 would get a bum deal while Unit 2 would receive a windfall. However, if the landlord based his rent reduction *on market value* to reflect the negative impact of the partial taking, then in this example, Unit 1 would receive a 75% rent reduction.

	Unit 1		Unit 2		Building	
	Sq.Ft.	Rent	Sq.Ft.	Rent	Sq.Ft.	Rent
Before	2,000	4,000	1,000	1,000	3,000	5,000
After	1,000	1,000	1,000	1,000	2,000	2,000
Difference	1,000	3,000	0	0	1,000	3,000
% Difference	-50	-75	0	0	-33	-60

Clearly, in a multi-tenant building each space should be appraised separately after a partial taking to assess the impact of the condemnation on individual units.

• **Restoration of premises:** If part of the property is "taken," no doubt some repair or modification work is going to be needed. The lease should assign responsibility to either the landlord or the tenant for getting it done. Usually the cost will be paid from the condemnation award. If there is a shortfall, the lease should state clearly which party pays it.

• **Cancellation of lease:** This is similar to "Termination of Lease" (provision 13.03). If so much of the property is taken as to render the premises useless, the lease can give either the landlord or the tenant the option to cancel—another point to be negotiated between the landlord and tenant.

14.03 TEMPORARY TAKING OF PREMISES (M)

This is far more likely with vacant land than with buildings. It is possible that a condemning authority could need to use a leased property for temporary access and egress to another site, or for road construction or some other public purpose.

The "condemnation of a leasehold interest" is called a "temporary" taking. It can be total or partial. When it occurs without condemning the "fee" interest also, or without a "sale in lieu of condemnation" (provision 14.06), typically the lease will not terminate. However, except for clauses relating to the payment of money, the default provisions are usually made inoperative while the tenant is out of possession.

In addition, the amounts due are generally adjusted to the average of some number of rental periods between the commencement date and the date of condemnation. This puts a lid on the tenant's upside rent escalators during the down period.

In exchange, the landlord may give the tenant the right to pursue an award against the condemning authority for damages, and limit the landlord's right of recovery to compensation for any reduction to the "reversionary" interest in the "fee" (the value of the property after the lease expires). If the tenant is required to "restore" the premises after the period of condemnation, the award for damages to the tenant should include restoration costs. Sometimes, this concession by the landlord is coupled with the requirement that the tenant assign award proceeds to the landlord to be held in trust as security for the tenant's performance of the still operative covenants of the lease.

14.04 LANDLORD'S OPTION TO TERMINATE (M)

Many leases give the landlord the exclusive right to cancel if more than a stipulated percentage of the building and/or common area is taken. The tenant should be given adequate written notice, and rents prorated to the date of cancellation (see provision 14.02 —under "Cancellation of Lease" subheading).

14.05   CONDEMNATION OF PARKING AREAS   (M)

In situations where parking is critical to the tenant's success (e.g. in a shopping center), a total *or* partial taking of parking facilities should have roughly the same consequences. The tenant will want a rent reduction, or perhaps a termination depending on the severity of the taking. The landlord can try to provide comparable parking elsewhere, and usually agrees to spend the amount of the award in order to ward off cancellation of the lease by the tenant.

14.06   SALE IN LIEU OF CONDEMNATION   (M)

Because eminent domain proceedings can be so costly and time-consuming, and because the power of the court makes condemnation virtually inevitable once the process is started, some owners agree to sell at a price comparable to that expected from a condemnation award, rather than endure the legal process. Where the tenant has the right to share in the proceeds, the tenant should be given access to the sales negotiations with the condemning authority.

GROUP 15

SALE OR FINANCING

LANDLORD'S POSITION:

Lenders insist that their mortgages supersede any other claim against the property, except taxes. In order for a landlord to obtain financing, before or after the lease is signed, the tenant's interest must be inferior to the lender's.

When a property is sold, the buyer expects the tenants to remain on the property. For this reason, the leases must be transferrable. And, when a property is sold the buyer also wants to know that there are no undisclosed agreements between the landlord and tenants.

TENANT'S POSITION:

If a landlord slips into foreclosure, the tenant's lease is vulnerable to cancellation. Title to the property will transfer to the lender, who in turn most often will elect to sell the property (lenders are in business to make loans, not manage property). Unless the lease itself is woefully inadequate, or the tenant is in serious default, cancellation seldom occurs. Everybody wants to keep a good tenant.

The tenant's best protection against lease cancellation through foreclosure is to investigate the financial stability of the landlord before signing the lease. In addition, although I have personally never seen it done, a strong tenant could insist on approving the financial summary of a prospective *buyer*. Interesting thought...

COMMONLY INCLUDED PROVISIONS:

15.01 TERMINATION OF LANDLORD'S LIABILITY (M)

Once a property changes hands, for whatever reason, the previous landlord wants no further responsibility for any of the lease provisions. The new owner assumes the lease obligations, unless otherwise specifically agreed with the previous owner.

15.02 SUBORDINATION & NONDISTURBANCE (M)

It may be impossible for the landlord to obtain financing without this lease provision. Lenders consider the lease to be a lien on the property. Absent a subordination clause, leases signed before a mortgage or trust deed could take precedence. Lenders want their lien to be superior to any others. Of course, any modification, renewal or extension of a mortgage is also subject to the same subordination provision.

However, the tenant may negotiate a *nondisturbance* clause providing that if the tenant is not in default, its lease will not be canceled in the event of a foreclosure. Major tenants will want this agreement in writing from the *lender* before agreeing to subordinate their lease to a mortgage.

15.03 ATTORNMENT (M)

Attornment means that a tenant agrees to accept a new owner as landlord. When a property is sold or exchanged, or if a ground lease is terminated before its term expires (other than by reason of condemnation or casualty loss), the lease is transferred by assignment to the new owner. Without this clause, the tenant could conceivably refuse to honor the new owner as landlord.

Also, as stated above, in a foreclosure action, if a mortgage is superior to a lease, as it almost always will be, the lender has the option to cancel or continue existing leases. This clause provides that if a lender notifies the tenant of its election to continue the lease, the tenant agrees to accept (attorn to) the new landlord.

15.04 ESTOPPEL CERTIFICATE (M)

Prior to closing escrow, a new owner or lender needs to know that the leases being transferred are valid. The tenant is therefore required to verify its lease with an "estoppel certificate," or an "offset statement," which is a written declaration by the tenant that the lease, and any acknowledged modifications to it, are in full force and effect. It verifies the commencement and termination dates, the amount of any prepaid rent, the date to which prepaid rent applies, and the amount of the security deposit. Finally, it lists the terms of any special agreements with the landlord, and contains a statement that there are no uncured defaults by the *landlord* to the best of the tenant's knowledge.

Since time is of the essence in closing a sale or loan, there is a time limit for returning the certificate to the landlord. Failure to comply is considered a default by the tenant, which invokes the default remedies, one of which is lease cancellation. Some leases even give the landlord a power of attorney to sign the certificate for tardy tenants.

15.05 OPTION TO BUY / RIGHT OF FIRST REFUSAL (H)

Occasionally, a large and financially strong tenant in a multi-tenant building, or, a strong tenant in a single-tenant building, will be able to negotiate an option to buy the property. This usually occurs only under a long-term lease, and/or if the tenant makes a considerable investment in interior improvements. Failing to acquire a purchase option, such tenants can sometimes negotiate a "right of first refusal," which entitles them to match the terms and conditions of a bona fide offer received by the landlord. Refer to provision 18.05 for a discussion of both situations.

GROUP 16

GENERAL PROVISIONS

LANDLORD'S POSITION:

This group is a "potpourri" of provisions needed to tie the other ones together, and take care of a good many "housekeeping" chores relative to the mechanical operation of the lease.

TENANT'S POSITION:

While these provisions can be scattered all over the lease, and, are generally not earth shaking in their content, they should be examined in the context of the tenant's individual circumstances. Things that don't apply, or that are impossible or impractical to comply with, should be modified or eliminated.

COMMONLY INCLUDED PROVISIONS:

16.01   PARTIES TO THE LEASE

Get the names right! **And I mean exactly**!! Sorry for the shouting, but you can't begin to imagine how many leases I've seen with the wrong names. It's so basic, yet *so* neglected. Find out if you are dealing with an individual, or a partnership, or a corporation, or some combination. Make sure the person signing the lease, on either side, has the legal authority to bind the entity to a contract. Ask for a copy of the partnership agreement, or a corporate resolution. When it comes time for the parties to sue one another, it *can* make a difference! "He who assumes, blunders."

16.02 PAYMENTS NOT TO BE WITHHELD

This clause states that if a dispute arises over rent, other amounts due, or any other provision of the lease, the tenant is to continue to pay required amounts until the dispute is resolved. The landlord should agree to refund any overpayments promptly, and to diligently pursue settlement of any such disputes.

16.03 BROKERS' COMMISSIONS

Brokers beware! "We're only a commission away from making the deal" is all too commonly heard at the end of sometimes long and arduous negotiations. All parties should have their commission agreements in writing, properly signed, and the consensus reiterated in the lease. It never ceases to amaze to me how many people develop amnesia when it comes time *to pay* commissions!

16.04 ASSUMPTION OF RISK / OTHER TENANTS

Refer to provision 10.05, "Contents Of Demised Premises."

16.05 QUIET ENJOYMENT

This provision is often glossed over and taken for granted, but it is actually a very significant clause. Quiet enjoyment means the right to use leased property without disturbance of possession by the landlord.

Easements, such as light and air easements, are *by law* included in the right of quiet enjoyment. For this reason, a provision reserving this easement to the landlord is usually included in the lease (see provision 1.03). Other easements, such as access and egress, are also considered part of the demised premises.

One of the tenant's remedies for the disruption of this right includes the right to file an action for breach of the covenant. A breach of this covenant by the landlord may also be used by the tenant as the reason for a counterclaim, or "setoff," against unpaid rents. For this reason, most leases include a provision for "waiver of counterclaims" by the tenant if the landlord sues for non-payment of rent (see provision 16.19).

The tenant and the landlord should be sure that the provisions of the lease, and the tenant's intended use, are in conformance with all provisions of any mortgage, ground lease, or "covenants, conditions & restrictions" encumbering the property. If the tenant can prove the loss of profits because of interference with the use of the premises, the landlord might be liable for damages. Finally, if a ground lease exists, the tenant should ask the landlord to state that, at the time of signing, the landlord is not in default under the ground lease, and that there is no imminent likelihood of a default, since the landlord's default could jeopardize the tenant's lease.

16.06   BANKRUPTCY—Insolvency / Landlord's Remedies

This was covered in provision 12.02, "TENANT'S DEFAULT."

16.07   NON-PERFORMANCE BY LANDLORD

This was covered in provision 12.01, "LANDLORD'S DEFAULT."

16.08   ATTACHMENT OF PREMISES / LIENS

This was covered in provision 12.02, "DEFINITION OF TENANT'S DEFAULT."

16.09 ATTORNEYS' FEES

Anyone can file a lawsuit against anyone for anything. The lease usually says the losing party pays the legal fees for *both* parties. Touché!

16.10 NOTICES

Throughout the lease, reference is continually made to one party giving notice to the other. Notices can be routine (rent past due), or extremely critical (condemnation notice). The name and address listed here should be that of someone likely to be there when a notice arrives, knowledgeable enough to interpret it, and conscientious enough to deal with it. An individual or partnership with a single location might prefer to use a home address; a corporation, its regional or home office; and anyone, their attorney's office.

16.11 LANDLORD'S PROCESSING COSTS

Many times, the tenant needs plans, specifications, or other documents from the landlord for construction, legal or other proceedings. This clause says the tenant can have all the help and documents from the landlord that he can afford!

16.12 ARBITRATION

Courts are overloaded. Jury trials are time-consuming. Attorneys are expensive. Consequently, litigation is costly. As a result, some landlords prefer to use arbitration to resolve disputes. The number and qualifications of the arbitrators, and how they are to be paid, is spelled out in this provision. Some issues may be excepted from arbitration; e.g., rent schedules or approval of plans and specifications.

Usually, the arbitration is "binding" on both parties, but some leases allow for an appeal through the courts. A tightly worded clause states that if statutes permit, a judgment may be recorded which is not subject to appeal. This clause is often used in lieu of a waiver of jury trial provision (provision 16.19).

16.13 DEMOLITION

Depending on the age and condition of the building, and the nature of competition in the marketplace at the time the lease is signed, the landlord may want to preserve the option to demolish the building and rebuild during the lease term. The key issues for the tenant are length of advance notice, reimbursement of unamortized improvements and trade fixtures, as well as costs of relocation. The tenant might ask the landlord to include a statement that at the time of signing there are no demolition plans for a given number of years.

16.14 ENCUMBRANCES— THE LANDLORD'S RIGHT

This was discussed in provision 12.02, "DEFINITION OF TENANT'S DEFAULT."

16.15 TIME IS OF THE ESSENCE

Most things in business run on some sort of schedule. Sales and loan escrows, legal notifications, and other business transactions operate on fixed time periods. Therefore, time is always of the essence relative to any provision of the lease.

16.16 GUARANTY OF LEASE

An "exculpatory clause" *limits* the liability of a tenant (or a landlord, or a borrower) to its interest in the subject property. A *guaranty* clause is exactly the *opposite*. If you are asked to guarantee a lease for a tenant, you must understand this provision.

Whether the entity is a partnership or corporation, a guaranty usually binds each signatory for the *total* liability of the lease, regardless of the amount of ownership interest. If there are ten partners on the guaranty and nine fail to pay, the tenth is still liable for *all* the money! That's what "jointly and severally" means. And, the landlord can go after any assets you own in the typical well-worded guaranty. Any and all! Bankruptcy, insolvency, or "I didn't know" will not absolve a guarantor from the responsibility for payment. (See Exhibit C.)

16.17   CANCELLATION—NOTICE TO MORTGAGEE

Lenders like to know that their mortgage payments will be made. If the building has a single tenant, or just several key tenants, the loss of one of them may seriously jeopardize the landlord's ability to pay the mortgage. To protect their position, most lenders insist on including this provision, which provides that if the *landlord* fails to cure a default, or commits an act interpreted by the tenant as eviction, the lender must be promptly notified by the tenant, and given a reasonable time to fix the problem before the tenant takes further action.

16.18   FINANCIAL DISCLOSURE

The landlord has the right to know the tenant's financial capability to handle all the rent payments and other responsibilities required under the lease. Either prior to or concurrent with submission of the lease to the landlord for signature, the prospective tenant must submit recent financial statements and/or credit reports for the landlord's review and approval.

16.19 WAIVER OF JURY TRIAL & COUNTERCLAIM

This provision states that the landlord and tenant both agree to waive a jury trial if either party commences legal action against the other for matters connected to the lease. The provision also asks the tenant not to file a counterclaim if the landlord sues for nonpayment of rent, but does not stop the tenant from filing a *separate* action against the landlord. (Refer to provision 16.05, "QUIET ENJOYMENT.") The idea seems to be to simplify the legal process. Again, whenever you are asked to waive a legal *right* it is wise to seek legal *counsel.* When the lease contains this provision, it will likely *not* contain an arbitration clause (provision 16.12).

16.20 RECORDATION

Since the lease is a transfer of property rights, the tenant might want its rights made part of the public record. The important point is that the act of "recording" gives public notice. It is not necessary to disclose the exact contents of the entire agreement. Therefore, a "short-form" lease is often used which states only the names of the parties, the description of the premises, and the commencement and expiration dates. Only a *recorded* lease is eligible for a "leasehold owner's" insurance policy (see provision 18.01–Title). Of course, the tenant can expect to pay for all costs connected with recording the lease.

A recorded lease will be considered an encumbrance on the property, and, third parties can record liens against a recorded leasehold. Therefore, many leases will prohibit recordation, especially when the landlord has not yet obtained permanent financing.

If it *is* permitted, a recordable release or reconveyance document is often required from the tenant, which is recorded upon lease expiration or termination to eliminate the encumbrance. Sometimes the provision grants the landlord a power of attorney to record the release if the tenant fails to record it within a given number of days after the lease ends.

16.21   COVENANTS & CONDITIONS

A "covenant" is an agreement to do or not to do something. The remedy for violation of a covenant is usually a suit for damages, or an injunction. A "condition" is a qualification on an estate, in this case the leasehold estate. The remedy for violation of a condition can be reversion of the estate to the creator of the condition. In other words, violate a covenant, you get sued. Violate a condition, you lose your lease!

To add more legal clout to the lease provisions, some leases contain a clause stating that *all* requirements of *each* party to perform will be considered both a covenant *and* a condition. Compliance with every provision then becomes critical.

16.22   SUCCESSORS & ASSIGNS

Unless a *covenant* "runs with the land" (meaning it has been "recorded"), it is not binding on successors in ownership. Therefore, most leases contain a provision that makes all covenants binding on successors in interest, because many leases are not recorded.

16.23   NO PRIOR AGREEMENTS

In the process of negotiating a lease, it is common to have a number of preliminary drafts, often for the same provision. This clause invalidates all but the *most recently signed* draft as representing the entire agreement between the parties.

16.24   NO ORAL MODIFICATIONS

Anything discussed during the negotiations must be reduced to writing to become part of the final lease agreement. "But you said," or "I remember you telling me" won't carry much weight in court. If it is not included in the lease you're pretty much out of luck.

16.25 LAWFUL MONEY

Few landlords want to be on the barter system. This clause says you can't pay rent with chickens or barley. It probably applies mostly to foreign tenants who deal in other than U.S. currency.

16.26 INVALID PROVISIONS

If legislatures or court decisions change laws or ordinances, or in the unlikely circumstance that the attorney made a mistake in drafting the lease, and a provision or something in a provision is found to be invalid, this clause says that the remainder of the lease is still enforceable.

16.27 GENDER, CAPTIONS

I don't know how people do business without this one! It says that "he" also applies to "she," "his" to "hers," etc. A lady landlord must have complained one time, so they all include this provision now.

And, just so you know, the words beneath the paragraph headings, and not the captions themselves, define the agreement. Your guess is as good as mine why that one is in there.

16.28 EXAMINATION OF LEASE

The tenant does not legally have a deal when the landlord submits a lease for review and signature. The landlord does not want to be tied up for extended periods while the tenant lollygags around reading the lease. Another tenant might make a better offer in their interim.

However, in the spirit of fair play toward the sincere tenant, I always ask the landlord for a few days notice if an offer is received from another potential tenant (see my "Offer to Lease,"—Exhibit B). Within that period the tenant can sign and return the lease if it has been under review for, say, five days or more. If the tenant has had an attorney working on a lease for *that* long, there ought to be some opportunity to complete the deal, or at least match the terms of another bona fide offer.

GROUP 17

RETAIL LEASE SPECIAL PROVISIONS

LANDLORD'S POSITION:

While the value of any property is influenced by its location, retail space has "franchise value." It has special value just because of its unique ability to generate traffic for the retailer. The problem is to determine "how much" the franchise value is worth (see provision 17.13).

Economic uncertainties in the 1930's depression popularized the "percentage" lease for retail property, and since World War II percentage rents have become the norm for shopping centers and "strip" retail centers along commercial thoroughfares. "Minimum" rents are estimated by the landlord to cover operating costs, ground rents if any, and debt service on loans. Percentage rents create the landlord's profit potential as the property matures and draws more sales volume.

Some tenants, banks for example, escape percentage rents because they draw considerable traffic to the center. Also, second story space is usually not attractive to retailers (due to presumably reduced foot traffic—except in malls) and it is often converted to office use, thereby skirting percentage rent. Leases for these tenants will normally contain periodic rent increases, or be limited to short terms, in order to give the landlord an opportunity to periodically increase rents.

TENANT'S POSITION:

While the percentage lease allows the tenant to minimize the "going-in" rent, the tenant is not guaranteed a profit just because rent is based on sales. Successful retailers know the numbers of their business. To ensure the success of the business, it behooves both the tenant and the landlord to keep the actual percentage of sales within a comfortable range of profitability, projected on the basis of sales dollars per square foot. Restaurants, for example, generally cannot operate profitably with rents above 8 to 10 percent of gross sales . A variety of publications list commonly used percentages for various types of businesses, or the tenant may consult a broker or appraiser. Astute landlords will be skeptical of tenants willing to pay above average rents.

COMMONLY INCLUDED PROVISIONS:

17.01   PERCENTAGE RENT   (H)

Percentage rents may be computed on "gross sales" or on "net profits." Because of the problems, and let's face it, the abuses that can crop up in computing "profit," most leases are based on the tenant's "easier to determine" sales.

There are several variations of the percentage-of-sales provision.

- **"No minimum; percentage only":** Very large retail chain stores will not readily agree to a minimum rent for a new and unproven location. They obligate the landlord to share the risk of developing the property's desirability by agreeing to pay a percentage only. Smaller retailers might get away with this type of lease on a secondary site, or in an extremely overbuilt market. The landlord must be careful that such deals do not impede financing, since lenders typically consider *minimum* rents as their security when underwriting a loan.

- **"Percentage against a minimum"**: This method provides the landlord *minimum rent* for coverage of operating expenses, loan payments, and ground rent, while still creating upside income potential from *percentage rent.* It also allows the possibility for escalating the *minimum rent* annually as operating costs increase, or as mortgage or ground lease payments escalate. This is probably the most commonly used method.

- **"Minimum plus a percentage"**: The *percentage* can be based on the total sales volume, or on sales in excess of a stated amount. The *minimum rent* can be fixed for the lease term, graduated periodically throughout the term, or conditioned on the tenant achieving specified sales volumes. Obviously, the exact combination must be negotiated. Only the most energetic landlord's use this type of lease.

Sometimes tenants try to negotiate a "cap" or limit on percentage rents. Needless to say, landlords resist this because it defeats the main purpose of the percentage clause — to protect the landlord against inflation, and create profit potential by sharing in the increased value of the site.

17.02   GROSS SALES DEFINED   (H)

Why dwell on this? Sales are sales. If you sell something it's a sale, right? Well, life is rarely so simple! Especially where human nature is involved, which means *greed* gets involved. If rents are based on "sales," doesn't that motivate the tenant to *understate* "sales"? Not that anyone would ever *do* such a thing, but the landlord does have to be cautious. (Remember, the difference between being "dishonest" and "clever" depends on your point of view!)

Not that anyone would ever *do* such a thing. . .

As a result, most retail leases contain heaps of language defining "sales." Provisions 17.03 through 17.13 (that's 11 provisions!!) deal with measuring, monitoring, and regulating "gross sales." Imagine how many it would take to do "net profits"!

Gross sales will typically include:

- the total value of any transaction made on the premises, or as a result of the tenant's occupancy of the premises.

- cash, credit, and gift certificate sales.

- no deduction is allowed for charges imposed by credit card companies.

- mail order and telephone sales, and orders from outside sales people working from the premises.

- sales originated from the premises but actually filled somewhere else (e.g., from a warehouse).

- sales resulting from license agreements originated from the premises.

- bad debts, premiums, trading stamps or other advertising and promotion costs are business expenses, and therefore are not usually deductible from gross sales.

There *are*, however, some permissible deductions:

- refunds for previously included cash or credit sales not exceeding the sales price.

- merchandise *transferred* among the tenant's stores merely to facilitate operations.

- sales or excise taxes absorbed by the tenant.

- gift certificates not redeemed where they are sold.

17.03 RECORDATION OF SALES—CASH REGISTERS (H)

Verification of gross sales starts at the point of sale. Most leases will insist on the use of serially numbered sales slips, and/or the use of cash registers or computers that display the amount of each sale and produce a tape and an unchangeable internal total. Maintenance and repair records are required when the machines need service in order to discourage tampering with the machines' totals.

17.04 REPORTS BY TENANT (H)

The lease will stipulate the day of the month by which gross sales reports are due to the landlord, and the form and content of the report detailing gross sales and percentage rent calculations. Sometimes there is a requirement to have the reports certified periodically by a public accountant—monthly, quarterly or annually. Most often the percentage rent *payment* is due with the report.

17.05 RIGHT TO EXAMINE TENANT'S RECORDS (H)

Key to enforcement of the percentage rent provision is the landlord's ability to inspect the tenant's books and sales records. The lease should spell out exactly which receipts, sales agreements, tax returns, and other documents are to be made available for inspection, where, at what times, and for how many years in the past.

17.06 AUDIT (M)

The landlord usually reserves the option to perform a sales audit at any reasonable time. The audit should be restricted to the tenant's business originating from the premises. The clause usually contains an interest penalty for verifiable underpayments of percentage rent. If the shortage exceeds a stated percent (1 or 2), the tenant may be required to pay for the audit, and/or for all subsequent audits (conducted at the landlord's discretion). If the deficit is larger, the landlord can have the option to cancel the lease upon short notice, sometimes as short as 5 days! Obviously, this is *not* a provision to be taken lightly.

17.07 ERROR ADJUSTMENT (M)

Some leases contain a separate provision stating that if an audit reveals an overpayment of percentage rent by the tenant, the landlord will either issue a refund, or apply the overpayment to future rents due.

17.08 REFUND OF TEST PURCHASES (M)

Landlords sometimes employ "shoppers" to monitor the tenant's conduct within the premises, especially the recording of sales. Merchandise purchased by shoppers is returned to the tenant for a refund, and deducted from gross sales calculations. The lease can impose a cancellation penalty if the tenant fails a stated number of shopping tests within a given time period. I know of one landlord who "shopped" a *prospective* tenant, then refused to negotiate a lease because the tenant failed to ring up the sale. Another provision not to be taken lightly!

17.09 MAXIMUM SALES EFFORTS (M)

Percentage rents will not be achieved if the tenant is not diligently operating the business. This provision imposes a duty on the tenant to keep the premises open for business during certain hours of the day and days of the year, to maintain adequate inventory levels, and to provide sufficient personnel to operate efficiently. Keep those doors open!

Sometimes there is a penalty formula for "additional rent" if the tenant fails to comply with the hours of operation. For example, the minimum daily rent is often doubled for the number of days of improper operation.

Another consideration, frequently contained in a separate clause, is restriction of the tenant's ability to operate *competing locations* within a certain distance from the leased premises, except for facilities existing on the date the lease was signed.

Sometimes, this provision calls for sales from new locations to be included in the calculation of gross sales at the original site, or else the lease may be terminated at the landlord's option! The nature of the tenant's business, the nature of competition in the area, and the perceived risk of rent loss to the landlord determine the particular constraints imposed.

Maximum sales effort!

17.10 LIMITATION ON TYPE OF MERCHANDISE (M)

"Tenant mix," designed to create synergism by assembling a variety of goods and services, is critical to the success of a retail center. Many times as a condition of signing the lease, a tenant negotiates the *exclusive* right to provide a product or service within the center. This requires the landlord to place a restriction in every other tenant's lease. Besides, without this provision, the landlord would have no control over *any* tenant's merchandising activities.

17.011 VENDING MACHINES (M)

Unless vending machines, video games, or the like are the tenant's principal business, the lease will usually require the landlord's prior written approval before their installation. Their physical placement on the premises and inclusion in the definition of gross sales are the principal issues.

17.12 RECAPTURE / RIGHT TO CANCEL LEASE (M)

Except for circumstances beyond the tenant's control (e.g., catastrophe; landlord's alterations; economic recessions), if percentage rent drops in any year by a set percent (say, 20 or 25), the landlord may reserve the right to give the tenant notice and terminate the lease. Of course, there is seldom a reciprocal right for the tenant to cancel.

17.13 NO PARTNERSHIP INTENDED

This clause clarifies that the intention of the percentage rent clause is only to provide a method for establishing the value of the property's location for determining rent, and not to create a partnership interest for the landlord in the tenant's business. Enforcing the tenant's adherence to provisions in the lease would be tricky if the parties were declared to be "partners."

17.14 ADVERTISING REQUIREMENTS (H)

Retail leases normally contain a provision requiring the tenant to spend a certain amount each year advertising *specifically its store* located within the landlord's property, in media approved by the landlord. Sometimes there is also a requirement to advertise directly *within* the leased premises. In both cases, the amounts are generally set as percentages (1% or 2%) of annual gross sales.

To enforce this provision, the lease requires the tenant to supply the landlord each year with a summary of amounts spent in each medium. The landlord usually reserves the right to audit such expenditures. If there is a shortfall, a contribution to the merchant's association or a payment to the landlord is stipulated in the lease.

17.15 ADVERTISING—NAME OF BUSINESS (M)

The landlord's percentage rent depends in large measure on the center's ability to attract and maintain an established clientele. Once a tenant gains significant market recognition, the landlord is reluctant to see any changes that might jeopardize the center's drawing power, including the name change of a successful tenant. Therefore, some leases require the landlord's approval for name changes.

17.16 ADVERTISING—SOLICITING IN COMMON AREA (M)

If every tenant were permitted to use the parking lots, mall areas, and other common elements for signs and banners, the center would look like a menagerie. The same holds true if every tenant could distribute hand bills throughout the center. The most effective way to prevent a tenant from abusing the common area is to prohibit every tenant from using it for solicitation.

17.17 ADVERTISING—PROMOTIONAL CHARGES (H)

Some landlords establish a program to promote the retail center as a whole. Funding for this program usually comes from an assessment to each tenant, commonly based on a square footage charge calculated to cover a prescribed budget. It is wise for tenants to look for a limit on the amounts chargeable for this fund; for instance, a certain percentage increase over the prior year.

While landlords will typically resist the attempt, tenants should also try to arrange for some *participation* in the use of the fund. Payment of this charge is considered to be additional rent, due on the day rent and other charges are due. Tenants need to put this charge into their "Occupancy Cost" budget (see Exhibit F).

17.18 MEMBERSHIP IN MERCHANTS' ASSOCIATION   (H)

The success of retail centers of any size depends heavily on the attitudes of both the landlord and tenants about the merchants association. Mutual cooperation is crucial in achieving the center's full sales potential. All tenants, including and especially the anchor tenant(s), should be required as a *condition* (provision 16.21)of the lease, to join the landlord in the association.

Dues are normally computed on the basis of "gross leasable area," collected with other rent charges, and should be included by tenants as part of their "occupancy cost" budget. Less common are formulas based on gross sales, front footage, annual rent, or individual negotiations.

Customarily, the landlord will contribute a percentage of the annual budget (usually 25), or, less commonly will match amounts contributed by merchants. Uniformity among tenants is important for administration and collection of dues by the landlord.

The association can be either a profit or non-profit corporation. Both have their advantages and problems. Serious tenants should insist on reviewing the organizational documents and bylaws of the association before signing a lease, as well as its standing committees (publicity, special events, finance, etc.). The merchants association plays a vital role in shaping the center's "personality," market image, and consequently the success or failure of each individual tenant.

17.19 APPORTIONMENT OF SALES PROCEEDS (H)

See provision 11.03—LANDLORD'S RIGHT TO PURCHASE.

17.20 EMPLOYEE PARKING (M)

Providing adequate and convenient parking is always a challenge. In the interest of providing convenient parking to *patrons* of the center, landlords generally reserve the right to restrict employee parking to certain areas, and to change these areas from time to time. Tenants often must provide license plate numbers of employees, and agree to indemnify the landlord if employees' vehicles are towed or a fine imposed for parking improperly.

17.21 EMPLOYEES' COSTUMES & CONDUCT (M)

A shopping center or resort is an integrated economic unit. Each tenant has a responsibility to maintain a positive public image for the center. To this end, some landlords place reasonable requirements on the tenants to control the conduct and appearance of their employees.

Each tenant has the responsibility to maintain a positive public image.

17.22 ENLARGEMENT OF SHOPPING COMPLEX (M)

In the event that the landlord obtains additional land, and/or constructs additional rentable area in the retail center, this clause usually provides that old and new tenants will be treated alike. Both will be subject to the same rules and regulations, and have the same rights and privileges.

Unless a mortgage prevents it, a common budget is generally created and each tenant's pro-rata share is recomputed based on the increased square footage. This is equitable unless the new improvements add excessive costs to the common area, or are available predominately to the new tenants by design. The landlord often retains the right to *rent* some of the additional parking spaces.

Tenants should investigate the likelihood of this provision being used during the lease term. Ask the landlord about future construction or remodeling plans, and inspect adjoining sites. If the probability is high that it could occur, adjust the language of this provision accordingly, perhaps negotiating a *limit* on the amount of such rent increases.

17.23 INSURANCE—FIXTURES & MERCHANDISE (H)

This provision requires the tenant to carry adequate contents insurance, and was covered also in provision 10.05— "CONTENTS OF DEMISED PREMISES." Quite obviously, an uninsured disaster can put a tenant out of business if merchandise inventory, furniture, and equipment cannot be replaced. The landlord would then be faced not only with the loss of rent while finding a new tenant, but also with possible brokerage commissions, legal costs, and renovation expenses.

17.24 RELOCATION—LIMITATION ON LANDLORD (M)

There are a variety of reasons why a landlord would want to relocate a tenant during the lease term. Perhaps the tenant has failed to achieve the expected sales volume for a choice location, but is still considered to be a worthwhile part of the center. Perhaps the landlord needs to "assemble" a large space for a new or expanding tenant, and another tenant is in the middle of two empty spaces. Or perhaps general renovation or expansion plans require moving a tenant elsewhere.

Leases commonly provide that in this event the landlord must give the tenant advanced written notice of the proposed new location (30 to 90 days). Fixed minimum rent is normally abated from the time moving starts until finished, but is usually limited to a certain number of days. The landlord usually will pay reasonable moving costs, which should include: the unamortized cost of interior improvements; labor for removal and reinstallation of fixtures and equipment; insurance premiums and "deductible" losses under the tenant's insurance policy; and the cost of printed, promotional, and advertising material committed to before the date of notification by the landlord. Finally, if the proposed space is significantly larger than the old space, the tenant is given the option to cancel the lease (see provision 11.06— NEGOTIATING A CANCELLATION).

17.25   SECURITY REQUIRED BY TENANT   (H)

Refer to provision 1.04,—"ALARM SYSTEM." Responsibility for security *inside* the leased premises rests with the tenant in most cases. Plans for installation of security systems usually need the landlord's approval, and the landlord also reserves the right to provide security guard service as a common area expense.

17.26   STORAGE—OFFICE SPACE   (M)

This provision appears occasionally, and states that the leased space is to be used *primarily for retail sales*, and any office or warehousing uses shall be incidental to the operation of the business. Office and warehousing don't generate as much percentage rent as retailing.

GROUP 18

GROUND LEASE SPECIAL PROVISIONS

LANDLORD'S POSITION:

The ground lease makes it possible for the landowner to retain ownership of the land but to create separate ownership of the improvements built on the land. Any type of property can be ground leased; residential, commercial, industrial, and resort.

Reasons for preferring a ground lease over a sale are as individual as the owners negotiating them. The property could be an extremely valuable and irreplaceable location, such as a downtown corner or a suburban shopping center. It could be a property that has been in the family for generations which, for sentimental reasons, no one wants to sell. Perhaps the owner needs to lease (rather than sell) for estate planning purposes, or to avoid harsh tax consequences from a sale, or to shift income to family members in lower tax brackets.

TENANT'S POSITION:

For the tenant, the ground lease is essentially a financing vehicle. Whether the tenant is the end-user or an investor/developer, the *landowner* will examine carefully the tenant's financial strength, credit history, and experience with the type of property under consideration—just as a lender would.

For a developer, projects which were not feasible with the full land cost in the pro-forma can become attractive when the land is leased. Paying only a security deposit instead of a sizeable downpayment significantly reduces initial capital requirements. And, because of the reduced capital requirement, ground leases allow a developer to tackle *additional* projects. Of course, since the developer becomes "landlord" to sub-tenants, the terms and conditions of the ground lease must provide the flexibility needed to accomplish the developer's marketing program.

A word of caution. A "short-form lease," or "memorandum of lease," should be promptly recorded as "constructive notice" for the *tenant's* protection. Without "actual notice" (via *direct,* verifiable communication), or constructive notice to third parties by "recording" in the public record, in most jurisdictions the ground tenant's position will not be protected in legal proceedings.

COMMONLY INCLUDED PROVISIONS:

Many of the provisions found in the commercial lease are also found in the ground lease. Those that do not apply are obvious; for example, "relocation of the tenant," "employees uniforms," "alarm systems," and so on. The approach to rent, taxes, insurance, assignment, default, condemnation, and other major provisions is similar for both types of leases. Accordingly, discussion of this group will concentrate on concepts and provisions *unique* to the ground lease.

18.01 TENANT'S INVESTIGATION PERIOD (M)

Investigate before you invest! Good advice when buying. Equally good advice when leasing. There are a number of important issues for a prospective tenant to consider before signing. If they are not resolved prior to signing, they should be made conditions for cancellation within the lease itself if study results are unsatisfactory. Each situation is different, so the "free look" period must be adjusted to fit the circumstances of both parties. The advice of experts should always be sought, and care should be taken to allow enough time "free of rent" to complete meaningful studies. "He who assumes, blunders!"

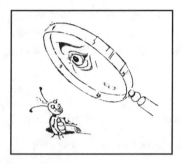

TITLE: Tenants should not assume that the landowner has valid title to *all* property rights. There could easily be a defect in the vesting claimed; a forged deed; a lien or other encumbrance not recorded; or a defect in an easement.

In 1975, the American Land Title Association devised a "leasehold owner's policy." It is available in many states and provides title insurance coverage to the tenant similar to a fee owner's title insurance. The policy includes a formula for valuing the leasehold estate. It also covers losses resulting from eviction due to a defective title, such as: moving costs; damage to personal property during the move; payments due to the true owner under the previous lease; and, damage to subtenants.

Premiums are based either on the value of the land and improvements, or, on the annual rent over the term of the lease. Endorsements are available at an additional premium for zoning violations, and for validating an option to purchase the fee.

The title company will usually require an appraisal of the leasehold, and insist on handling the escrow for the lease transaction. Only *recorded* leases qualify for the coverage. Any tenant contemplating a sizeable investment on leased land would be well-advised to investigate the availability of such an insurance policy.

The tenant should always order a preliminary title report from a title insurance company, or have an abstract of title done by a competent attorney. All encumbrances should be investigated, and specific attention devoted to:

- the location of **easements** which might impede development and need to be relocated,

- deed restrictions on **use** of the property

- **mortgage clauses** which might interfere with intended development plans

The total amount of mortgages relative to the value of the property, and, the total debt service (loan payments) in relation to proposed ground rent should also be ascertained. If the landowner's mortgage payments are too high, and equity too thin, the tenant could be moving into a very precarious position on an overburdened property on the brink of foreclosure (15.03).

CROPS: In some cases, construction might have to be delayed because of crops in the field. I remember one developer who had to postpone closing on a site in an *industrial* park until a farmer harvested his tomatoes!

SOILS TEST: Site work can be very expensive. If the compaction is not right for the proposed construction, the excavation, removal and importing of proper soils can ruin a budget estimate. It's even more expensive if the condition is discovered after the construction fails!

Toxic contamination is another good reason to conduct soils and ground water tests. A host of laws and government regulations make it very unpleasant for land owners with contaminated soil. If there is a problem, you definitely want it documented or corrected *before* committing to a long term lease. Federal laws such as the "Resource, Conservation, and Recovery Act," and, the "Compensation and Recovery Act" (the "Superfund" of 1980) can require clean-ups costing millions of dollars! Astute lenders are increasingly insisting on a soils test as part of the loan package. Basic analysis can usually be done for several thousand dollars. Check the yellow pages under the headings "environment" or "soils testing" for companies providing the service.

I walked away from a ground lease on an outstanding corner gas station site once because of soils conditions. We wanted to build an office building. The owner was a major gas retailer, and wanted *us* to agree to rectify any *potential* contamination (solely *our* cost) discovered by a soils test which *we* would buy. Sure!

I remember another owner whose tenant had installed a gas pump beside the building. In order to get a building permit for the next tenant's renovations, the pump had to be removed, and a soils test done. *Several months later* the owner was still paying to have the entire parking lot excavated, uncontaminated fill dirt imported, the lot repaved — and the contaminated soil hauled in specially-approved trucks hundreds of miles away for disposal!

SURVEY: Wouldn't you just hate it if you got all finished with your office or industrial building, or even a shopping center, and your neighbor stopped by to tell you your building was on part of his property? It's called "encroachment," and it isn't very funny. So hire a qualified surveyor to verify the boundaries shown on the title report. And be sure somebody *reads it* (like your architect and civil engineer)!

We built a shopping center once and found out that our roof line extended a few feet into our neighbors proposed driveway. It turned out that the architect never had, or couldn't find, a copy of the survey. It cost us $20,000 to pave our neighbors driveway, a couple of month's time, and attorney's fees to get an easement for our roof! We didn't think so then, but we probably got off cheap! Do a survey!!

ZONING/RE-ZONING: The permitted uses on a property are dictated by local zoning ordinances. Unpermitted uses will require a variance, a use permit, or straight out re-zoning in order to accomplish the tenant's goals. Many times, a developer will tie up a parcel with the intention of getting it re-zoned to a higher use (called "downzoning," for some reason). During the investigation period, the developer must assess his chances of winning the politics of the re-zoning process. It can be very time-consuming, and as a result, very expensive.

Setbacks, building-to-land coverage ratios, and parking requirements are also controlled by zoning ordinances. These restrictions dictate how much leasable space a site can produce. They should be researched during the free-look period to verify the economics and financial feasibility of the proposed project.

GOVERNMENTAL APPROVALS: Time is money. If the tenant plans to construct or redevelop a building, a thorough understanding of the time required to get through the planning and building permit processes, as well as through any other agencies (e.g. environmental protection agencies or other state or federal regulatory agencies), is key to a profitable project. As mentioned, a variance, use permit, or re-zoning can add "oodles" of time to a project. Sometimes it takes weeks just to figure out which agencies are *involved* in the approval process. Market conditions can change while you are in the "grist mill," and turn the economics of your deal upside down!

ASSEMBLAGE / RECIPROCAL EASEMENTS: Investigation of the site will reveal the need, if any, for acquiring access to (or through) adjacent parcels. This is important. It can make or break a proposed development! Access and egress, site planning, building dimensions, parking ratios, and even permitted uses can be affected by the availability of additional land.

When additional property is deemed necessary, it can be assembled by purchase, lease, or easement. The signing of the primary ground lease must be conditioned on closing escrow on the other purchases or leases, or singing of easement agreements. Except for a purchase, the negotiations will include settlement of the distribution of condemnation awards issue.

Where the lease method is chosen, and where different property owners are involved, it makes sense to use separate leases with separate rent schedules on the separate properties, but *without* cross-default clauses. Watch the site plan, and be careful to preserve the separation of property lines.

Easements, of course, "run with the land" (which means they're transferable) so they take precedence over the ground lease and any mortgages on the property. Resolving the easement issue facilitates negotiations for the ground leases and financing agreements. It could become impossible to obtain financing without the easements if their existence is considered crucial to the success of the project by the lender. The lender will also want to know the *costs* of maintaining or operating the easements. You will need a competent civil engineer and attorney to help with easement negotiations.

UTILITIES / FUTURE ASSESSMENTS: The location, adequacy, and financing of all utilities to the property must be determined early in the investigation period. The landlord must agree to grant utility easements when they are needed in order to induce the utility companies to make capital expenditures for the property. If *the municipality* decides to finance utility installation through a bond issue (and add the cost to the property tax bill), the lease must state whether the landlord or tenant pays the assessments.

The location of existing utility easements should be drawn over the proposed site plan to uncover the need, cost, and feasibility for easement relocations. We had a great shopping center piece under contract one time in a joint venture with a bank. It happened to be triangular, surrounded on three sides by city streets. (We were actually *buying* the land, but the problem is the same either way.) During our investigation period, we found that the city wanted to condemn one of the streets and give the land to the adjoining owners, which was good (because we were one of them)! But they also decided to require us to convert the overhead electric and telephone lines to underground, which *wasn't* so good. Then we discovered we had to share the "free" street land with the adjoining landowner, so we had to negotiate a utility easement with him, but he had no development plans, which was *bad.* It took so much time that during the negotiations the market turned down, everybody lost interest, we ran out of money, had to sell the property, and lost all the money we had invested in studies, which was *really* bad!

SUMMARY: Establish a realistic period for feasibility studies, and use the time wisely. Each of the topics listed above should be addressed in detail. Since the cost of preliminary studies is normally borne by the tenant, it is reasonable to expect the landlord to forego rent for an adequate period of time, and to modify the language of the ground lease to address the problems and peculiarities discovered during the investigation.

For example, extensions of time to complete studies, rent reductions, or even cancellation could be required if extraordinary conditions are uncovered. On the other hand, it is reasonable for the landowner to expect good faith deposits periodically as the investigation progresses through predetermined benchmarks. The more thorough the investigation studies by the tenant, the greater the likelihood of a successful project.

18.02 CONSTRUCTION OF BUILDINGS   (H)

The landowner has a vested interest in the success of the development. As a result, the ground lease requires the landlord's approval of plans *prior* to starting construction. The process for approval and turnaround time should both be stated, plus a prohibition against the landlord being arbitrary and unreasonable with his approval.

The tenant will normally negotiate the right to add additional buildings, or modify existing ones. The landlord will insist that alterations or demolition shall not diminish property value. Commonly, the landlord requires performance bonds on contractors and subcontractors, as well as indemnification of the landlord against the tenant's liability arising during construction.

To protect against building code changes *subsequent* to completion of construction, the lease should provide that a tenant's construction, done in accordance with approved plans, will be deemed to comply with applicable codes and laws. The tenant should also seek indemnity against non-conformance of *existing* improvements with current building codes.

Most often, the tenant will be required to obtain the landlord's permission to remove existing signs. In exchange the tenant will insist on being exempted by the landlord from liability resulting from their removal, in case the sign locations were leased to an advertising company.

Most often, the tenant will want to establish the right to ownership and depreciation of improvements built on the property. The ground lease should also cover the issue of reversion of ownership, or, removal of improvements, upon expiration of the ground lease.

18.03 FINANCING / SUBORDINATION (M)

Subordination makes the *land,* as well as the improvements, security for loans against the property leased. The subordination provision of a ground lease is similar to the one discussed in provision 15.02, except the *landowner* must agree to subordinate the ground lease for the *tenant's* benefit. Subordination is key to the tenant obtaining financing, since most lenders are prohibited from making *leasehold* loans if the lease is inferior to a *prior* mortgage on the *fee.* And financing is the key to a project's development. No financing, no project!

To be effective, the subordination clause should also *prohibit* the *landowner* from placing a mortgage, lease or sublease in a *priority* position over the *tenant's* lease or mortgage. Frequently, the landlord will be restricted from placing *any* mortgage on the fee until a number of years after lease commencement or recordation, and/or only if the *landowner's lenders* agree to execute subordination agreements with the *tenant's lender,* thus giving the tenant's construction or permanent lender priority. Some leases also place a ceiling on the amount of mortgage the landowner can create. In any event, the encumbrances are restricted to placement on the owner's *fee* interest *only.*

What this means is that if the tenant's lender is not put in first lien priority through subordination agreements from the landowner, there will be no financing. No financing, no project!

While most landlords understand the need for subordination, they don't always like it. The landowner's primary risk is foreclosure on his *fee* interest if he is unable to forestall a *leasehold* mortgage foreclosure. If the owner lacks the financial ability to make payments on the leasehold mortgage should the tenant default, the tenant's lender *could* sell the property in foreclosure for the amount of the tenant's unpaid loan balance or less, most likely leaving the landowner empty handed!

Consequently, the financial capability of the tenant, and the equity (market value minus loans) remaining after financing is put in place, is crucial to inducing the owner to subordinate his interest in the ground lease to potential leasehold mortgages. The owner has every right to require a detailed credit and financial history of the tenant, and subtenants, early in the negotiations. The tenant's expertise and financial strength is the landlord's best insurance for subordination.

Other inducements for the landowner to subordinate the fee to the ground lease include:

- signed sublease(s) from anchor tenant(s) with strong financial statements

- a significant earnest money deposit from the lessee— nonrefundable is better than refundable

- a joint venture agreement with the owner (sometimes in exchange for lower rent), where the owner participates in the development profits

- higher than usual rent

The owner can further safeguard his subordination by placing a dollar *limit* on the amount of a *leasehold* mortgage placed on the property. The limit would usually be the amount of the original construction loan. In this case, the tenant could be required to seek and pay for a "loan commitment" for the specified amount from an owner-approved lender.

The loan commitment requirement would force the tenant to prepare site, floor, and elevation plans, building specifications, utility and other easements, a title report, the ground lease with a subordination clause, subleases or letters of intent, and a marketing plan with the proposed tenant mix. The time and expense of producing all this will test the tenant's sincerity — and patience; and pocketbook! With a loan commitment in hand, the landowner's risk at the time of signing the ground lease is significantly reduced. The tenant is almost "doomed to succeed."

In addition, the landowner could require a paydown or payoff of the leasehold mortgage after a number of years, or, after the owner grants renewals or extensions of the ground lease. The owner could also bargain for periodic increases in the ceiling on *fee* interest mortgages, thus allowing the landowner to withdraw equity. Finally, the leasehold mortgagee (lender) can be required to apply the proceeds of insurance or condemnation awards to reconstruction of the improvements, instead of retiring the loan, as additional security for the landowner.

Despite the use of various inducements, some landowners will still refuse to subordinate their land. In this case, there is a different set of provisions needed in the subordination section.

• There will be a specific *prohibition* against encumbering the landlord's *fee* interest with a *leasehold* mortgage. Only the improvements (not the land) will be security for the tenant's loan. Or, if encumbering the fee *is* allowed, the *leasehold* mortgage will be required to be secondary to the *fee* interest mortgage.

- No leases will be modified or canceled without the consent of the leasehold mortgagee. Construction and permanent lenders will want this protection.

- The leasehold mortgagee (lender) will be given the option to cure the ground tenant's default, and to operate the property in lieu of the tenant.

- The leasehold mortgagee will be given the option to negotiate a new lease directly with the owner upon the tenant's default.

A leasehold mortgage is difficult to obtain without subordination, but without *these* protections in an *unsubordinated* ground lease, the tenant has virtually *no* chance to secure financing. No financing, no project!

Subordinated or not, under a sale/leaseback agreement in which a ground *lessee sells* its interest to an investor, and then *leases* the property back, most ground leases will require the *original* tenant to remain *primarily* liable to the landowner under the ground lease. Also, lenders will look for the ability to succeed a bankrupt or insolvent tenant who slips into default, and to operate the property to protect their loan. Both of these provisions should be made part of any ground lease agreement.

18.04 NON-DISTURBANCE AGREEMENT (M)

Under this provision, the landlord agrees not to disturb the tenant's right to quiet enjoyment, and subtenants, despite the ground tenant's breach of lease, cannot be evicted *if* they are in compliance with the lease covenants (opposite of "merger," provision 11.04). While this may be repugnant to the landlord who may have little or no control over sublease agreements, without it the tenant will not be able to attract subtenants because they would have no control over their destiny on the property. There are a number of compromise alternatives.

The lease can require the landlord to accept subtenants *approved by the lender. Net worth* standards can be defined for all sub-tenants. *Minimum space* sizes, *minimum* fixed and percentage *rents* for various tenant types, and limits on the *length of fixed rent periods* can be established and audited by the landlord.

Of course, these become restrictions on the tenant's marketing flexibility, so they must be negotiated carefully.

18.05 PURCHASE OPTION (H)

Because the ground tenant usually makes an enormous investment of time and money in the property, most often an option to purchase the fee will be sought. Indeed, for the landowner eager to attract a quality developer or user-tenant, the option to buy is an attractive carrot. The purchase option allows the parties to tailor the price, and the method of payment, to their individual needs.

The lease should spell out the date(s) on which the tenant may exercise the option, or series of options. This allows both parties to plan for the event, and to control the tax consequences of the transaction. A variety of pricing schemes is available to the parties. For instance, the price can be set as a fixed amount, an amount escalated by some formula (such as a cost-of-living index adjustment), or a "market" amount based on an appraisal at the time of exercise.

The length of time between the commencement date of the lease and the option exercise date(s) will dictate which method is best. For short periods, a fixed amount will probably work.

As the time period lengthens, the owner will want the inflation protection of an escalation formula, or a current appraisal.

The option provision should specify the condition of title to be delivered by the owner — what *encumbrances* will be removed or remain. In addition, the length of the escrow period, and the allocation and proration of closing costs should be detailed. Sometimes an entire purchase agreement is attached to the lease as an exhibit to eliminate uncertainties about the details of the option agreement.

If the owner absolutely refuses to grant a purchase option, a fall-back provision for the tenant is a "right of first refusal." The owner will *not* be *obligated* to sell, but if a bone fide offer arises, the tenant will be given an opportunity to match its terms and conditions for a stated period of time.

While few tenants go to the trouble, it's a good idea to have a contingency plan for exercising a purchase option or right of first refusal. Financing arrangements should be reviewed periodically with a lender, and perhaps an appraisal updated occasionally.

18.06 LEASE OPTION (H)

Many development projects, because of market conditions, their size, or their complexity, must be completed in *phases.* The landowner can reduce the risk of the developer's non-performance by using a lease option, or "rolling" option. The option can be inserted in the ground lease, or contained in a separate agreement.

Before the lease is signed, the developer is required to present a master site plan showing the phased areas, accompanied by building plans, financing plans, a list of required governmental approvals, and a timetable for implementation. The lease option then converts the developer's promises into specific "conditions" (see provision 16.21) for exercising the option for the land needed for each phase. If the "conditions" are not met, the option is canceled, and the landowner is able to continue on with someone else. This adds a degree of risk for the tenant, but remember, the landlord operates under the "Gold Rule"!

CONCLUSION

The commercial lease is an intricate and complicated document. It controls the quality of a landlord's investment, and the security of his income stream. It controls the personality of a retail center, the sophistication of an office complex, the image of an industrial park. It has tremendous legal and economic consequences on both landlord and tenant. Needless to say, both parties should seek competent real estate counsel at the outset. Find a real estate *specialist*, not someone who "dabbles." There is far too much at stake.

It would be nice if the "standard form lease" really were "standard." I am certain it would then be easier to teach people how to read, interpret, and negotiate it. Perhaps someday attorneys will agree on "standard groupings" for the various standard provisions. Perhaps someday they will adopt *mine*.

I must re-emphasize one point. The key to "digesting the lease" is to identify the "key words" of the various provisions. Key words will be scattered and disguised, sometimes cleverly, sometimes clumsily, but always verbosely. *Find and group them!* Strip away the legalese by referring to the related provisions in this book, and make sure the lease says what you want it to say.

Conclusion

The objective of this book has been to create a concise summary of the salient points of the lease for landlords, tenants, and other parties involved in lease negotiations. Perhaps negotiations will be easier because the parties better understand not only the issues, but also each other's points of view. For the novice, this book should eliminate some of the fear and anxiety that possesses each and every one of us who has ever confronted that monster legal document for the first time!

I learned some things by writing this book, and I sincerely hope you learned something useful from reading it. I wish you the best of luck in your lease negotiations. Perhaps we will meet during a transaction somewhere along the way!

If you have any suggestions for revisions, would like to know about future publications planned, or make arrangements for a speaking engagement, please send your name and address to:

Thomas G. Mitchell
MACORE INTERNATIONAL
PO Box 10811
Lahaina, Hawaii 96761-0811
FON/FAX (808) 669-7463

EXHIBIT A

SAMPLE TABLE OF CONTENTS

•Importance of "grouping"—compare groups with paragraphs
•Your lease should be numbered like this before you start reading

STANDARD FORM COMMERCIAL LEASE

GROUP	PARAGRAPH	PAGE
16	1. Quiet Enjoyment	1
16	2. Parties	1
1	3. Premises	1
2	4. Rent	1
3	5. Term	1
7	6. Security Deposit	2
2	7. Payment Of Rent	3
2	8. Additional Rent	3
12	9. Interest And Late Charges	4
16	10. Attorney's Fees	4
2	11. Landlord's Expenditures	5
5	12. Taxes On The Property	5
8	13. Alterations	6
8	14. Liens	7
8	15. Repairs And Maintenance	9
10	16. Insurance And Indemnity	11
13	17. Fire And Damage	12
9	18. Common Area Maintenance	14
1	19. Security	17
9	20. Parking	18
6	21. Utilities	19

Exhibits

Exhibit A *[continued]*

EXHIBIT B

OFFER TO LEASE
(Example)

OFFER DATE: January 1, 19__

NAME OF APPLICANT: Tenant's Full Name

ADDRESS OF APPLICANT: Tenant's Correct Address

CONTACT PERSON: Name and Phone Number

BLDG. & STORE #:   Address & Unit Number

FLOOR AREA (APPX.):   Approximate SQ. FT.

USE OF PREMISES: A concise, but accurate description of the tenant's proposed use of the premises.

LEASE TERM: Number of years, plus, the option period(s) desired, if any.

RENT SCHEDULE: (Initial Term)

Year	Base Rent
1	$ *
2	$
3	$

* Payment of rent shall commence upon Applicant's receipt of building permits for needed interior improvements.

If Applicant cannot obtain permits within 90 days after execution of lease, Applicant shall have the option to cancel the lease and be refunded the security deposit.

OPTION TERM: Base rent to be adjusted at the beginning of the first option year by the percentage difference in the Consumer Price Index from the start of the first year of the initial term and the end of the third year of the initial term.

ESTIMATED COMMON AREA CHARGES: Applicant agrees to pay its proportionate share of common area charges, a budget for which Landlord shall provide Applicant prior to execution of the lease.

SECURITY DEPOSIT: Applicant shall pay Landlord a security deposit of (usually one month's rent) upon execution of the lease.

TENANT IMPROVEMENTS: Landlord shall deliver the demised premises to Applicant in the condition existing at the time of execution of this Offer To Lease, including:

Store Front	Air Conditioning	Demising Walls
Electric Panel	Interior Paint	Convenience Outlets
Wood Floor	Stubbed Utilities	Ceiling & Lighting

Applicant shall submit plans for proposed improvements & fixturing prior to commencing build-out.

FINANCIAL STATEMENTS: Applicant shall submit current financial statements and three bank references upon submission of the lease to Landlord for execution.

NON-COMPETITION: Landlord shall include in Applicant's lease a covenant prohibiting its right to lease space in the building to any other (Applicant's type of business) tenant.

SPECIAL CONDITIONS: Should Landlord decide to relocate the Applicant, Landlord shall give Applicant written notice of its intention to do so. Applicant shall within 30 days notify Landlord of its decision to move to the new location, or to terminate this offer.

Should Landlord construct additional new space as part of the Center, or, upon the land on which the demised premises are a part, if Applicant is at that time in good standing, Applicant shall have a right of first refusal on such space.

EXECUTION OF APPLICATION: Until such time as the Landlord's lease is executed by Applicant and received by the Landlord, and a good faith deposit made, Landlord shall have the sole right to offer the premises to others and entertain offers on the premises.

However, once the Landlord has submitted the lease to Applicant for review and signature, and a period of ten business days has elapsed after such submission to Applicant, Landlord shall give Applicant at least three business days advance notice of its bona fide intention to sign another lease for Applicant's premises.

APPLICANT: (Full Name of the Tenant)

BY: _____

        (Full Name of Person Signing)

TITLE: _____

DATE: _____

EXHIBIT C

GUARANTY OF LEASE
(EXAMPLE)

Whereas (name of landlord), hereafter referred to as landlord, has agreed to enter into a lease dated (date of lease) with (name of tenant), hereafter referred to as tenant, for the premises located at (address of property), and,

Whereas landlord requires as a condition of executing said lease that the undersigned guarantee the performance of the tenant under said lease,

Now therefore in consideration of the execution of said lease by landlord, the undersigned hereby unconditionally guarantees the full performance of each term, covenant, and condition[1] of said lease by tenant, including the payment of all rents and other amounts that may become due thereunder. The undersigned further agrees as follows:

1. That this covenant shall continue in favor of landlord through any extension, modification, or renewal of said lease by the parties thereto, or by their successors or assigns.

2. That this guarantee shall continue unchanged by any bankruptcy, reorganization, or insolvency of the tenant or any successor or assignee of the tenant, or by any disaffirmance or abandonment by a trustee of the tenant.[2]

3. That landlord may, without notice, assign this guarantee in whole or in part and no assignment or transfer of the lease shall operate to extinguish or diminish the liability of the undersigned.[3]

4. That the liability of the undersigned shall be primary, and that landlord may commence an action against the undersigned without having commenced an action or obtaining a judgement against the tenant.[4]

5. That the undersigned will pay reasonable attorney's fees and other costs incurred by landlord in any action to enforce this guarantee.

6. That the undersigned hereby waives notice of any demand by landlord, as well as any notice of default in the payment of rent or other amounts due under said lease.[5]

7. That the obligation of two or more parties hereunder shall be joint and several,[6] and shall be binding upon and inure to the benefit of the respective successors and assigns[7] of the parties named herein.

_____   _____
(NAME OF GUARANTOR)   DATE

AUTHOR'S NOTES:

1 — see provision 16.21, Covenants & Conditions
2 — see provision 16.06, Bankruptcy or Insolvency
3 — see provision 15.03, Attornment
4 — see provision 16.16, Guaranty of Lease
5 — see provision 12.03, Landlord's Remedies
6 — see provision 16.16, Guaranty of Lease
7 — see provision 16.22, Successors & Assigns

EXHIBIT D

AGREEMENT OF CANCELLATION
(EXAMPLE)

This agreement is made and entered into this _____ day of
_____, 19__, by and between (name of landlord),
hereafter referred to as landlord, and (name of tenant),
hereafter referred to as tenant.

Whereas tenant and landlord have entered into a lease dated
_____, 19__, for the premises known as (address of
the premises), and

Whereas landlord and tenant desire to cancel, surrender, and
rescind said lease and the leasehold estate thereby created, and
to release each other from any and all further obligations under
the provisions thereof,

Now, therefore, it is mutually agreed:

1. That as of _____, 19__, said lease is
   hereby canceled, surrendered and rescinded, and
   the leasehold estate thereby created terminated; and

2. That all rights and obligations of landlord and
   tenant in connection with said lease, or any
   provision thereof, shall be and the same are forever
   settled, and landlord and tenant are hereby
   discharged from any and all of their respective
   obligations thereunder, subject to the following
   conditions:

CONDITIONS OF CANCELLATION:

_____

_____

_____

_____

_____

_____

_____

_____

_____

_____

_____

_____

_____

_____

_____

_____

BY: (Name Of Tenant)   BY: (Name Of Landlord)

DATE: _____   DATE: _____

EXHIBIT E

Ten Ways To Collect $5,000 Per Month For 36 Months

THERE ARE FOUR STEPS:

1. Determine the amount that needs to be adjusted
2. Determine the options available to both parties
3. Determine the priorities of both parties
4. Use your imagination and fashion a compromise

1. KEEP IT SIMPLE:

Charge the tenant $5,000 per month.

2. GRADUATED RENT SCHEDULE:

Months	Amount	Total	-or-	Months	Amount	Total
1- 6	$ 1,000	$ 6,000		1-12	$2,500	$ 30,000
7-12	3,000	18,000		13-24	5,000	60,000
13-18	4,000	24,000		25-36	7,500	90,000
19-24	5,000	30,000				
25-30	6,000	36,000				
31-36	11,000	66,000				
AVG.	$ 5,000	$180,000		AVG.	$5,000	$180,000

3. EXCESS TENANT IMPROVEMENTS OVER STANDARD ALLOWANCE:

A) Assume the space is 1,800 square feet

B) Assume the standard allowance is $10 per square foot

C) Assume the tenant needs $30 per square foot, or, $20/sf excess x 1,800 sf = $36,000

D) Assume base rent with the standard allowance is $3.33 per square foot x 1,800 sf = $6,000 per month

E) $36,000 divided by 36 months = $1,000 per month in excess TI's

F) Tenant's "effective" rent is $6,000-$1,000 = $5,000.

4. FREE RENT:

A) Assume landlord needs "scheduled" rent of $6,000 per month for his loan. Total rent for 36 mos. = $216,000

B) Assume tenant insists on paying only $5,000 per month. Total rent = $180,000

C) $216,000 less $180,000 = $36,000 difference

D) $36,000 divided by the $6,000 "scheduled" rent = 6 months free rent required to average $5,000/month

E) Proof: 30 months x $6,000 = $180,000 divided by 36 months = $5,000 per month. Magic!

5. DEFERRING COMMON AREA CHARGES:

A) Assume "scheduled" rent on a "net" lease of $6,500 per month, but tenant's budget is $5,000 for 3 years

B) Assume real estate taxes are $6,000 per year, or, $500 per month average

C) Assume casualty insurance is $3,000 per year, or, $250 per month average

D) Assume maintenance costs are $9,000 per year, or, $750 per month average

E) If the landlord pays B), C), AND D), the tenant's "effective" rent is $6,500 less $1,500 = $5,000...

6. LANDLORD PAYS TENANT'S MOVING COSTS:

A) Assume "scheduled" rent of $6,000 per month

B) Assume tenant's estimated moving costs are $36,000

C) $36,000 divided by 36 months = $1,000

D) $6,000 less $1,000 per month credit = $5,000 per month average over three years. More magic!

7. LANDLORD PAYS TENANT'S ARCHITECT FEES:

A) Assume "scheduled" rent of $5,500 per month

B) Assume the tenant is to pay for interior improvements, and architect fees are $25,000

C) Assume the landlord agrees to pay $18,000 worth

D) $18,000 divided by 36 months = $500 per month

E) $5,500 less $500 = $5,000 per month

8. LANDLORD ASSUMES TENANT'S OLD LEASE:

A) Assume "scheduled" rent of $5,000 per month for the first 18 months, and, $6,000 per month for the last 18 months = $198,000 total rent

B) Assume the landlord takes over payment of the tenant's current lease of $3,000 per month for 6 months=$18,000

C) Tenant pays $198,000 less $18,000 = $180,000 over 36 months = $5,000 per month

9. LANDLORD PAYS TENANT'S UTILITIES:

A) Assume the following rent schedule:

Year 1 @ $3,500 per month = $ 42,000

Year 2 @ $5,500 per month = $ 66,000

Year 3 @ $7,500 per month = $ 90,000

TOTAL $198,000

B) Assume 5,000 sf with utilities = $.30/Sf

C) 5,000 sf x $.30 = $1,500 Per month

D) If the landlord pays the tenant's utilities for the first year, the tenant's "rent" is reduced $18,000

E) $198,000 less $18,000 = $180,000 divided by 36 months = $5,000 per month "effective" rent

#10. COMBINATIONS !!!

A) You're on your own!

B) "Mix and match" the techniques shown above

C) Choose the items in the proportions that meet the needs of both the landlord and the tenant. Create your own methods. Use your imagination and have some fun!

EXHIBIT F

OCCUPANCY COST ANALYSIS

(Hypothetical Example)

(Name Of Tenant)
(Address Of Premises)
(Date Prepared)

ASSUMPTIONS:

      Base rent equals percentage rent*
      Landlord bills tenants monthly **
      Total Square Feet   2,100

BASE RENT:

Months	1 - 6	$0.00
Months	7 - 12	$1.50
Months	13 - 24	$1.75
Months	25 - 36	$2.00

Base Yr."CAM" Chgs/Sf/Mo (Increase @ 5%/Yr) $ 0.91

Percentage Rent On Gross Sales	8.0%
Advertising Charge (% Of Gross Sales)	1.5%
Merchant's Assn. Fee/Sf/Mo (Incr. @ 5%/yr)	$ .10
A/C Charge/Unit/Mo; 6 Units (Incr.@ 5%/Yr)	$25.00

*   If *actual* sales volume exceeds *base* (minimum) rent sales levels, total rent will increase by the *percentage* applicable to *each item* times the *excess* sales.

**   The following spreadsheet would have to be modified to allow for a quarterly or annual billing frequency.

Expense Item	Months 1-6	Months 7-12	Months 13-24	Months 25-36
Base Sls.(Base/%)	$0	$39,375	$45,938	$52,500
Base Rent	0	3,150	3,675	4,200
Advertising. Chg.	0	591	689	788
Merchant's Assn.	210	210	210	210
A/C Charge	150	150	158	165
Parking Fees	0	0	0	0
"CAM" Charges:	1,911	1,911	2,007	2,107
R.E. Taxes	Incl.	Incl.	Incl.	Incl.
Casualty Ins.	Incl.	Incl.	Incl.	Incl.
Liability Ins.	Incl.	Incl.	Incl.	Incl.
Maintnce. Costs	Incl.	Incl.	Incl.	Incl.
Plate Glass Ins.	100	100	100	100
Occupancy Cost (per month)	$ 2,371	$ 6,112	$ 6,839	$ 7,570
Occupancy Cost (per sq. ft.)	$ 1.13	$ 2.91	$ 3.26	$ 3.60

Please note that occupancy costs as a percent of sales will decrease if some cost items are "fixed" (not based on sales).

This spreadsheet can be designed in a monthly "cash flow" format, or to provide "average annual" cost analysis. What should be apparent is that the analysis will have to be customized for each lease. For example, occupancy costs could be calculated at various sales volumes, and some items in this example might not apply at all.

As this example illustrates, each lease must be reviewed carefully to identify every item of cost, and the spreadsheet designed accordingly. As you can see, there is a big difference between "base rent" and "total occupancy costs," and that is the point of this exhibit!

GLOSSARY

A

Abstract of Title: A condensed history of a property's ownership showing all the links in the "chain of title" (the chronological changes in ownership) and a list of all liens or other encumbrances.

Alterations: Major modifications to the structural and/or non-structural members of a building, including the interior floor plan.

Arbitration: A process designed to allow parties to a controversy to settle their differences outside of the court system. The "Arbitrator" is one or more persons selected by both sides who hears their evidence and renders an "award." The decision may be "binding" and prohibit an appeal through the courts, or, "non-binding" which permits an appeal.

Assemblage: The incremental value derived from assembly.

Assembly: The act of acquiring ownership, or other rights to use, adjacent parcels of land. Making one big piece out of a bunch of smaller ones.

Assessed Value: The valuation of a property by a tax assessor for the purpose of levying taxes.

Assessment(s): Amounts levied against a property by a city or county, usually for improvements to the infrastructure.

Assignment: In real estate, a transfer of *all* of a parties rights and obligations under a contract. In a *lease* assignment, the new tenant becomes primarily liable to the landlord, and the old tenant is relieved of *all* its lease obligations. The lease remains unchanged, and is simply appended as an exhibit to the "Assignment of Lease" agreement.

Glossary

Assumption: Taking over the legal obligations under an existing contract, or, becoming a "Guarantor" for the payments under a contract.

B

Bankruptcy: A legal proceeding in which a debtor petitions the bankruptcy court for protection of its assets from its creditors.

Basis: "Cost basis" is the value assigned to property (land and buildings in the case of real estate), at the time of acquisition. The building value is used for determining depreciation deductions during the holding period. "Adjusted Basis" includes certain additions, alterations, and depreciation deductions made or taken during the holding period, and is used to compute gain or loss upon ultimate disposition by sale, exchange, or through condemnation or destruction.

Building-To-Land Coverage: The proportion of the land that is covered by the "footprint" of a building. Usually this ratio is determined by city or county zoning ordinance, and limits the size of single-story buildings. See also, "Floor Area Ratio."

C

Cap Rate: An abbreviation for "Capitalization Rate." Capitalization is the process of establishing the value of an "income stream" from an asset. The formula is: *NET* INCOME divided by PRICE. If PRICE is *unknown*, NET INCOME divided by the investor's DESIRED RATE OF RETURN will produce the PRICE.

Certificate of Occupancy: A legal notice posted at a jobsite by a contractor and approved by the building department showing that all items included in the building permit have been satisfactorily constructed. It is often used to set the commencement date for rent or occupancy in a lease.

Condemnation: The taking of private property by a public agency through the right of "Eminent Domain" for a public purpose upon the payment of just compensation by the agency to the owner. Also, the declaration by a local building department that a structure is unfit for use and occupancy.

Consideration: *Anything* of value given or promised by one party to induce another to enter into a contract. Money, personal property, a promise to do or not to do something.

Constructive Notice: See "Recordation."

Cross-Default Clause: A provision in a mortgage, ground lease, or easement affecting a parcel of "assembled" property which makes a default under *one* contract a default under *all other* contracts in the assembly.

D

Debt Coverage Ratio: A calculation used in determining loan amounts. It computes the number of times annual net income exceeds annual debt service (loan payments). The formula is: Annual Net Income divided by Annual Debt Service. The lower the required ratio for a given income, the higher the loan amount, and vice versa.

Debt Service: Loan payments on a mortgage, trust deed, or any other form of loan.

Demised Premises: Demise means to transfer or convey. In leases, the landlord conveys the premises to the tenant, thus creating a leasehold estate, or, the demised premises.

Developer: In real estate, an individual or entity who acquires property, designs site and building plans, obtains financing, building permits, and construction contracts, then leases, and usually manages the property until its ultimate disposition.

Glossary

Double Net: In a "net" lease, the stipulation that the tenant pays two of the following three expenses: real estate taxes, insurance, or maintenance costs.

E

Early Occupancy: See "Possession."

Easement: A right to use another owner's land for a specific purpose, such as access or egress, or for the construction of utility lines. When properly "recorded," easements are said to "run with the land," meaning they are transferable.

Eminent Domain: The right of the government to acquire private property for public ar quasi-public use, and the right of the owner to fair compensation, as provided by the Fifth Amendment of the United States Constitution.

Encroachment: Construction of improvements on an adjoining property. For example, a fence; driveway; or building.

Encumbrance: Anything that limits or reduces the use, transfer, or value of real property, or that places restrictions on the fee simple title. "Money encumbrances" are called "liens"; a mortgage or trust deed, for example. "Non-money encumbrances" include easements, zoning laws, or covenants, conditions and restrictions. All "liens" are encumbrances, but not all "encumbrances" are liens.

Escalation Clause: A provision in a contract (mortgage; trust deed; ground lease; etc.) providing for increases in payments or interest rates based on specified contingencies; such as, an increase in an interest rate index, or an adjustment in the base ground rent.

Execution: The physical act of "signing" a legal document. Also, the act of performing, or carrying out, the duties and obligations of a contract that has been signed.

Extended Coverage: A casualty (accident) insurance coverage, usually associate with "fire" insurance, which insures against risks beyond fire damage, such as; windstorms; hurricanes; explosions, etc. Contact your insurance agent for a detailed explanation.

F

Fee: Also referred to as fee simple, fee interest, or fee ownership. The most complete degree of ownership of real property, free of all encumbrances.

Floor Area: The total area in a building, or leased space, usually measured from the mid-point of the thickness of one wall to the mid-point of the opposite wall.

Floor Area Ratio: In multi-story buildings, the total square footage of all floors divided by the total square footage of the lot. Usually determined by city or county zoning ordinance to control the "density" of lot coverage.

Floor Plan: An architectural drawing showing the perimeter walls, the dimensions and location of interior partitions and rooms, and the location of structural support columns within the walls. For "shell" space containing *no* interior improvements, a floor plan must be drawn and then built. For existing space, the floor plan must be drawn, then modified to fit the new tenant.

Foreclosure: A court proceeding whereby the holder of a mortgage or trust deed reclaims ownership of a property.

Franchise Value: In *retail* real estate, the inherent economic value of the location itself. Franchise value is best evidenced by the drawing power of the location in terms of sales. The landlord is usually compensated for it by percentage rent.

Free Look: An investigation period given to a prospective tenant by a landlord, during which the landlord cannot lease the property to anyone else, but the tenant does not pay rent while determining the suitability of the property for its use.

G

Gold Rule: "He who has the gold makes the rule." In this book, it is used to describe the landlord/tenant relationship.

Gross Lease: A commercial lease in which the *landlord* actually *pays* the costs of real estate taxes, insurance, and maintenance and includes their cost in the periodic rent.

Ground Lease: A lease of the *land only* to a tenant who will usually construct any needed improvements.

Ground Rent: Ground rent is usually based on a percentage of the periodically negotiated or appraised value of the land.

Guaranty: A legal document in which an individual (Guarantor) agrees to perform *all* obligations of a tenant or subtenant under a lease.

H

Hard-Money: A phrase referring to lease clauses which *definitely require the payment of money* by the tenant, and should therefore, be negotiated first.

Hazardous Material: Also "toxic" materials which cause "contamination" to a building or to land. They are important in the discussion of "soils tests."

Hidden Agenda: In negotiations, the "other party's" *undisclosed* reasons for wanting to make the deal.

Hold Harmless: To indemnify, or to secure another party against damage or loss.

Holding Over: Maintaining possession of a property after the lease term has expired.

Hypothecation: To pledge an asset as security for an obligation, without actually giving up possession of it.

I

Impasse Provision: A clause in a commercial lease stipulating the procedure for establishing option period rent if the landlord and tenant cannot agree on the amount during the option negotiation period.

Improvements: Generally, anything built on land. The building shell, the interior improvements, the paving and landscaping, the underground sewer and utility systems, streets, curbs, and gutters. Called "offsite" improvements when constructed by an owner on "dedicated land" (streets), and "onsite" improvements when constructed on private property. See also, "Tenant Improvements."

Indemnity: See "hold harmless."

Inflation: An increase in general price levels caused by an increase in the money supply and/or credit availability relative to the supply of goods available for purchase.

Insolvent: The inability to pay one's debts that are enforceable by law.

Interference: A term coined by the author to mean the many distractions in this world, mental and physical, disrupting one's ability to concentrate on what is being said.

J

Jointly and Severally: A legal expression meaning that the parties so bound to a contract are collectively (jointly) and individually (severally) liable for *all* the obligations under that contract, *regardless* of their proportion of ownership interest.

Glossary

K

Key Money: The amount paid to a landlord by a tenant as an *inducement* to enter into a lease. Most common in "high-franchise-value" retail locations. Also known as "incentive" or "premium" rent. Can sometimes amount to seven figures!

"Kick-Out" Clause: In a retail lease, a provision stipulating that if the tenant does not achieve a certain sales volume within a certain time period, one or both parties has the option to cancel the lease.

L

Land Coverage Ratio: See "Building-To-Land Coverage."

Lease: A contract between a land owner (landlord) and a tenant, specifying the terms and conditions upon which the tenant may use and occupy the property, and the length of time.

Leasehold: Also called "Leasehold Estate." The tenant's "legal right" to use and occupy a property during the term of the lease. Since it is a "right," it is personal, not real, property. Subject to restrictions negotiated in the lease, it is saleable and transferrable, and can be mortgaged (used as security for a loan).

Leasehold Mortgage: An instrument pledging a leasehold as security for a debt. Most commercial leases restrict such mortgages to securing only debts arising from improvements for the leased premises.

Leasehold Owner's Policy: A title insurance policy designed by the American Land Title Association in 1975 to insure a leasehold estate owner's interest in real property. The cost, coverage, and availability of the policy should be investigated before a tenant signs a lease.

Letter of Credit: A letter purchased from one's bank, used as security for a loan or a lease, stating that the customer will receive, if needed, a loan (credit) of a specified amount.

Lien: A money encumbrance on specific property (real or personal), making the property security for the satisfaction of a debt, or the performance of an obligation.

Lien Release: In leases, usually associated with "Mechanic's Liens," or, "Leasehold Mortgages." A document executed by the contractor or tenant, and recordable by the holder (landlord) when the debt is satisfied, to extinguish a previously *recorded* lien.

Liquidated Damages: A clause in a contract which stipulates the actual amount of damages to be collected by one party upon a breach of contract by the other.

Load Factor: In an office building lease, the percentage of non-rentable space (lobbies; restrooms; corridors; etc.) charged pro-rata to each tenant on the basis of square footage rented.

Load-Bearing Capacity: The pounds per square foot which a roof or floor can hold without caving in. (I hate it when that happens!)

Loan Commitment: A (sometimes difficult to obtain) written agreement from a certain lender to make a loan of a certain amount, at a certain interest rate, for a certain term, for a certain number of points, under certain conditions, as of a certain date — for a very certain commitment fee. Can be for either a construction or a permanent loan.

M

Mechanic's Liens: A statutory lien, filed by contractors, subcontractors, or material suppliers to real property, reverting back to the date the work or material was actually supplied. See "Notice of Non-Responsibility."

Mechanical: Refers to the heating and air-conditioning elements of a structure.

Merchant's Association: In retail or shopping centers, a (profit or non-profit) association of merchant-tenants formed by the developer or owner, to finance the promotion of the center as a whole.

Minimum Rent: In a commercial lease, the base, fixed rent applicable for a certain time period. Can be subject to adjustment periodically, based on negotiated terms.

Mortgage: A legal instrument which makes specific real property security for the payment of a loan, or the performance of an obligation. It sets forth a fixed procedure for "foreclosure" by the "mortgagee" (lender) if the "mortgagor" (borrower) defaults in satisfying its obligations.

Multi-Tenant: A property occupied by, or leased to, more than one tenant.

N

Needs: As used in this book, the points of negotiation absolutely necessary for the deal to be made by both parties. See "Wants."

Net Lease: Opposite of "Gross Lease." A lease in which the *tenant* is responsible for direct payment of taxes, insurance, and maintenance costs — as well as rents. Can apply to single-tenant or multi-tenant properties.

Net Rent: The rent under a "net" lease. The tenant can also be responsible for payment of "additional rent," such as percentage of gross sales, or excise taxes on rent paid to the landlord.

Non-Competition: A clause in a commercial lease prohibiting a *landlord* from leasing space to a subsequent tenant engaged in the same business as the tenant signing the lease, and it prohibits a *tenant* from opening competitive locations within a specified geographic area or distance from the demised premises.

Non-Disturbance: A lease provision that forbids the landlord to unnecessarily interrupt the tenant's business operations. It relates to the "Quiet Enjoyment" provision, and also says that if the tenant defaults, subtenants may continue in possession if they are in compliance with their contracts.

Notice of Completion: A legal notice posted at a jobsite by a contractor which starts a 45-day period after which no *new* mechanic's liens may be filed by laborers or material suppliers. See "Mechanic's Liens."

Notice of Non-Responsibility: A legal notice which, when recorded and posted at a jobsite by a property owner, relieves the owner from unauthorized materials or work supplied to the property. See "Mechanic's Liens."

O

Occupancy Cost: The *total* cost of leasing a premises, including: minimum rent; percentage rent; taxes; insurance; maintenance; parking fees; advertising fees; merchant's association fees; and any other charges assessed on a periodic basis. See Exhibit F.

Occupancy Rate: A calculation used to measure the effectiveness of the landlord's marketing program. The opposite of 'vacancy rate.' The percentage obtained when *total leased square footage* is divided by *total rentable square footage*.

Option: A right given for "consideration" (something of value) by a landlord to a tenant to buy or lease a property under specific terms and conditions for a specific period of time, without obligating the tenant to exercise the right.

Ordinances: Laws passed by local governments (either cities or counties).

Glossary

P

Parking Ratio: The percentage of the total number of parking spaces in relation to the total rentable area of a building, Usually stated in "number of spaces per thousand square feet" of building area. Minimum ratios are established for various uses by the local planning department to restrict building density, and they significantly impact the economics of a development project.

Partial Taking: The condemnation of only a portion of an entire property by a government agency for public use. For example, taking part of a parking lot to provide for street widening.

Percentage Rent: The rent charged a tenant under a percentage lease, usually based on gross receipts. Different percentages apply to different types of tenants.

Performance Bond: A bond purchased by a contractor at the insistence of a landlord as insurance for the timely completion of a job and the satisfaction of all debts and mechanic's liens related to it. See also, "Surety."

Permitted Uses: Property uses which *comply* with local zoning ordinances.

Possession: In leases, giving or taking of occupancy of the demised premises. Can occur before (known as "early occupancy"), concurrently with, or after the commencement date of the lease, or the commencement date for payment of rent.

Posturing: As used in this book, a negotiating principle wherein the parties establish their *ostensible* reasons for wanting the deal. See "Hidden Agenda."

Power of Attorney: A written document giving an agent the authority to act on behalf of a principal. Can be "general," covering a broad range of activities, or "specific" limited to strictly defined acts.

Preliminary Title Report: A report similar to an abstract of title, prepared by a title insurance company after an escrow is opened, "preliminarily" showing the current ownership and all recorded encumbrances against the property which will be included in the title insurance policy issued at the close of the escrow period.

Premises: The actual land, or space in a building, leased to a tenant. The property should be accurately described, and an exhibit showing a sketch of the premises included in the lease.

Prime Lease: The original, or earliest-dated lease. Sometimes called a "master" lease, the expression is used to distinguish it from a sublease.

Pro-rata Share: The proportion of costs allocated to a tenant in a multi-tenant property. Taxes, insurance, and common area maintenance are usually allocated by the percentage that a tenant's rentable square footage bears to the total rentable square footage of the property.

Proforma: A financial projection based on stated assumptions about future events. Income and expenses are portrayed in a format that shows the proforma author's expectation about the prospects for a proposed venture.

Property: Land, and any improvements built thereon, are considered "real" property. Everything else is considered "personal" property.

Q

Quiet Enjoyment: The right of a property owner, or a tenant, to use the property without interference from the other party, so long as they are in compliance with all the terms and conditions of their agreements.

R

Re-Zoning: A governmental procedure used for changing the zoning of a parcel. The applicant is usually interested in changing the zoning to a "higher," more profitable use. Re-zoning is often the motivation for property acquisitions.

Recapture: In *leases,* the negotiated right of a landlord to re-take a space from a tenant who does not meet performance standards specified in the lease for sales volume or rent. In *taxation,* addition to the owner's "adjusted basis" upon disposition of depreciation charges taken during the holding period. In *investments,* the process of recovering the cost of an investment by using a rate "of return" to establish the recovery period.

Reciprocal Easement: An agreement, usually recorded, between adjacent property owners to use certain portions of each others property for specified uses, for a specified period, under specified terms and conditions, for specified consideration.

Recordation: Recording. Placing a legal document on public record, usually by the County Recorder, which is said to give "constructive notice" to interested parties of the existence of an "encumbrance" to the property. Priority is usually given to claims based on the *date and time* of recordation of the document.

Redemption: In leases, curing a "default." In purchases, buying back one's property under a "judicial foreclosure."

Referenced Statutes: In most leases, for the sake of brevity, references are made to various "statutes" — laws passed by any of a multitude of legislative bodies— which become binding on the parties signing the lease.

Relocation: In a commercial lease, the negotiated right of a landlord to move a tenant from one location to another within a building or complex.

Remedies: The avenues of redress available to a party to a (lease) contract upon default by the other, provided either by the contract itself, or by law (statutory remedies).

Rentable Area: The square footage in a property for which the landlord can charge rent. Generally, the total area less common areas, such as; corridors, stairways, restrooms, utility rooms, etc. Also called "Net Rentable Area." See "Total Rentable."

Repairs: Routine maintenance of the non-structural elements of a building. (See "Alterations")

Retention Payment: An amount (usually 10% of the contract) held by an owner from a general contractor, or by a general contractor from a subcontractor or material supplier until the expiration of the mechanic's lien period (45 days after performance), to insure that any discovered defects are remedied.

Reversion: The right of a person, or the person's heirs, to future "possession" after expiration of the current estate; e.g., a leasehold estate.

Right of First Refusal: In a lease, the negotiated right of a tenant to match any bona fide offer received by a landlord to lease the demised or other premises; or, if negotiated, the right to match an offer to purchase the property.

Rules & Regulations: Most often, an exhibit to a lease describing important aspects of operation of the building or complex, such as; hours of operation, noise abatement, parking regulations, delivery procedures, trash removal, etc.

Run With the Land: An expression meaning that certain *recorded* documents, such as easements, become part of and are transferrable with title to the land.

S

Section: A fixed 640 acre parcel of land, established by government survey, and always "one mile square" (not necessarily the same as one square mile).

Security: *Physically,* preventive measures designed to forestall theft or vandalism. *Financially,* assets hypothecated or mortgaged to ensure the performance of obligations under a contract.

Setbacks: The front, rear, and side distances a structure must be placed from adjacent property lines, streets, or curbs as stipulated by the planning department, and enforced by the building department. Intended to control density of development, and to create aesthetic ambiance in neighborhoods.

Setoff: A legal term, wherein a tenant will endeavor to offset (setoff) a landlord's claim for rent based on a default of the landlord.

Shell: The four walls, roof, floor, pavement and landscaping of a building, with utilities "stubbed" to the walls. Interior improvements are specifically *not* included. Many buildings are leased in this condition.

Shopper: In retail leases, people hired by a landlord to make purchases in a shopping center and check if the tenant is accounting for every sale.

Short-Form Lease: For the purpose of "recordation," a *memorandum of lease* containing the parties' names, addresses, and the starting and ending dates of the lease will suffice to provide "constructive notice."

Single-Tenant: A property leased to only one tenant.

Site Map: An architectural drawing showing the property lines and the size, location, and dimensions of each structure on the parcel, as well as the location of landscaped areas, driveways and sign locations.

Soils Test: A study conducted by extracting core samples of earth from strategically located areas around a construction or other site, then examining them for composition, compaction qualities, and/or for the presence of toxic contamination.

Special Provisions: An exhibit containing all the terms and modifications to the standard provisions of a lease needed to customize the document to a particular deal. It is attached for ease of reference.

Standard Form Lease: The name given to the lease containing the customary provisions used by the landlord. There are as many "standard" leases as there are attorneys drafting them, or landlords using them!

Structural Elements: The members of a building constituting its "shell," including the foundation, floor, walls, roof structure and roof, sewer lines, water mains, and utility systems from the street to the building.

Sublease: A lease given by one tenant (lessee) to another tenant (sublessee). The original tenant remains primarily responsible to the landlord, and the subtenant is responsible to the original tenant.

Subordination: An agreement by the holder of an encumbrance on a property (mortgage; lease; ground lease; etc.) allowing certain rights to become secondary or inferior to another encumbrance.

Subrogation: *Substituting* one party for another with regard to a legal right or obligation.

Surety: A person who guarantees the performance of another. Hence, in a "surety bond" the underwriter (insurance company) guarantees the performance of the holder. See also "Performance Bond," and "Guaranty."

Surrender: Cancellation of a lease by mutual agreement of the landlord and tenant.

Survey: The process of establishing the exact boundaries of a parcel, measuring it, and determining its exact area.

Glossary

T

Tenant Improvements: Also called "interior improvements." Modifications to leased property required by the tenant. Can be inside or outside of the structure, and can be paid for by the tenant, the landlord, or both.

Tenant Mix: In retail real estate, the concept of putting together a homogeneous group of tenants in a center so as to create synergism and drawing power.

Term: The stated length of time during which a lease is valid.

Termination: Ending or canceling a lease for any reason.

Total Rentable: The total area of a building for which rent can be charged if there were only *one* tenant. Usually *includes* entry ways, corridors, restrooms, stairways, elevators, storage areas, and other parts of a building not used exclusively by one tenant. See "Rentable Area."

Toxic: Poisonous, or producing a poisoning effect.

Trade Fixtures: Items of "personal" property, affixed to "real" property by a tenant, which are needed to conduct its business, and are removable by the tenant. See "Property."

Triple Net: A commercial lease expression which says the *tenant* directly pays the costs of property taxes, insurance, and non-structural maintenance. In an "absolute net" lease, structural maintenance is also the tenant's responsibility. The "contract" rent is stated *exclusive* of these costs.

Trust Deed: A legal document which pledges real property as security for a loan. (Some states use "mortgages.")

U

UCC1: Uniform Commercial Code Form 1. This document serves a purpose for "personal" property similar to that of a mortgage or trust deed for "real" property. It pledges *personal* property as security for debt, and provides public notice of the lien.

Usable Space: The actual square footage available for the tenant's use. The square footage for which the tenant is charged, less the allocation for non-rentable areas. See "Load Factor."

Use Permit: A document obtained by a petition process, usually through the planning department of the city or county in which the property is located, after public notice and a series of hearings. It is required when an owner or tenant wants to use a property for a purpose not permissible under the zoning ordinance. Generally issued for a short period of time with a periodic renewal requirement.

V

Valuation: The estimated value or price of a property.

Variance: A document obtained through a process similar to that of a "Use Permit." However, a variance is a more permanent exemption from the zoning ordinance, and is for a specific feature. For example, a height limitation variance, or a parking variance.

W

Waiver: Relinquishing the privilege to enforce a right.

Wants: As used in this book, the negotiating points which the parties would *like* to win, but, are not absolutely essential to making the deal. See "Needs."

Glossary

Z

Zoning: The body of city or county ordinances specifying the allowable uses for each type of property. It also defines the boundaries within which such uses are permitted.

INDEX

Index

Index

Index

ORDER FORM

(please feel free to photocopy)

NAME: _____

ADDRESS: _____

CITY: _____ STATE: _____ ZIP: _____

PHONE: _____

Please send the following order. I understand that if I am not
fully satisfied with the book, I may return it for a full refund.

NUMBER OF BOOKS: _____ × $19.95= $ _____

SALES TAX:
Add 4% for books shipped to addresses in Hawaii. $ _____

SHIPPING:
Book rate: $2.00 for first book
75 cents for each additional book
(Surface shipping may take four to six weeks) $ _____
                        OR
           AIR MAIL: $3.00 per book $ _____

                                    TOTAL $ _____

PAYMENT

Check or money order, made payable to:

MACORE International
PO BOX 10811
LAHAINA, HI 96761-0811   **Mahalo for your order!**

SAN 297-6609